To Whom
the
Wilderness
Speaks

Books by Louise de Kiriline Lawrence

To Whom the Wilderness Speaks

Louise de Kiriline Lawrence

Drawings by Aleta Karstad

McGraw-Hill Ryerson Limited

Toronto Montreal New York St. Louis
San Francisco Auckland Bogota Guatemala Hamburg
Johannesburg Lisbon London Madrid Mexico New Delhi
Panama Paris San Juan São Paulo Singapore
Sydney Tokyo

To Whom the Wilderness Speaks

Copyright © Louise de Kiriline Lawrence, 1980. All rights
reserved. No part of this publication may be reproduced, stored
in a retrieval system, or transmitted, in any form, or by any
means, electronic, mechanical, photocopying, recording, or
otherwise, without prior written permission of McGraw-Hill Ryerson
Limited.

1 2 3 4 5 6 7 8 9 10 D 9 8 7 6 5 4 3 2 1 0

Printed and bound in Canada

Canadian Cataloguing in Publication Data

Lawrence, Louise de Kiriline, date-
     To whom the wilderness speaks

ISBN 0-07-092400-7

1. Birds – Ontario. 2. Birds – Behavior.
I. Karstad, Aleta, date- II. Title.

QL685.5.05L38   598.29713   C80-094493-3

Introduction

My husband and I intruded upon a piece of near virgin land about 12 years before my first nature story made its appearance in *Audubon Magazine* (New York). I use the term "intrude" intentionally, for, contrary to my early belief in my own ability to blend with the wilderness and benefit it, through the years I have come sadly to realize that the presence of civilized man, no matter how he strives to become totally adjusted, in some way inevitably disrupts the deep harmonies of the natural environment.

The land we chose was typical in character of the Canadian Shield – rough, rocky, unyielding and magnificent. And there we built our home. Any particular desire to gain first-hand knowledge about nature was not the immediate motive then. Rather, I was primarily looking for fresh air, space to move, for unadulterated solitude, time to think. To live the simple life in a small loghouse in an uninhabited forest, I thought, is freedom. Only later came the serious involvement with nature; it was pushed to the fore by circumstances. It was born out of the dawning realization that what I was seeing and hearing in these surroundings, what inevitably I was coming into contact with from day to day, becoming aware of, was something far more significant, far more vital, than anything I had previously known, or imagined, or expected.

I called this the opening of the portals. The process was slow, painstaking, and spread across half a lifetime. It is not yet at an end. It produced feelings of elation. To be able to see what before I could not see aroused surprise, excitement. The heart beat stronger; glints lit the eye. There was also bafflement. Insignificant as was the beginning, yet beyond it a world was foreshadowed indescribably vast and manifold. Unable to grasp it, I lived in a state of frustrated ignorance. Yet it existed and the growing awareness of its being, even in that initial moment of discovery, was overwhelmingly real.

So, gradually, the road led me from ignorance to revelation. And then, as my relationship with the natural environment deepened and was purged, the confusions overwhelmed me, the confusions of knowing more at the same time as I became acutely aware of knowing far too little of all there was to know to achieve understanding and attunement. My endeavours to understand better the immediate natural world in which we lived and shared have succeeded only insofar as recognizing a natural balance with all its enigmatic vagaries and logical effects as the mainspring of existence. But that, perhaps, is the most important thing of all.

Contents

Part One

The First Involvement

It would be inappropriate not to mention at this point the two eminent Canadian men of science who came to have great influence over the direction my involvement with nature would take. Their memorable characters will always stand out among the finest I have known and I am forever grateful for their contributions in the shaping of my thoughts and vision.

I never met either of them. The relationship developed entirely from the written word, of which both were masters. Only superior perception and wisdom are capable of inspiring the particular kind of humility of spirit that was the distinguishing characteristic of both men. It was my good fortune to be given so early in what I may call the second part of my life the opportunity to come in contact with each of them. And their response always allowed most generously for the continuation of our association over many years, in fact until their deaths.

A friend gave me the book entitled *Birds of Canada*, by P. A. Taverner, then curator of ornithology at the National Museum of Canada. Already filled with eager curiosity, I read the book from cover to cover. Annotated lists are not usually inspiring reading, but this one was different. Here the descriptions of the birds, such as ducks, hummingbirds, swallows, their habits and idiosyncracies, were given a literary treatment that turned them into gems. In spite of the need to adhere to a set form, a prodigious accumulation of knowledge so saturated the recorded references with first-hand personal experiences as to create vividly fascinating stories out of avian orders, families, and species. Delicate drawings by the author's pen of birds' bills, their feet, the fine texture of their downy feathers disclosed not only the differences that separated one species from the other, this subspecies from the next, but also an artistry that betrayed the illustrator's intimate knowledge of his subjects.

I wrote an enthusiastic letter to him. To my surprise, an answer came. And this was for me the beginning of a strangely edifying friendship and an educational period where nature, birdlife and philosophies of nature were ever so gently imprinted upon my mind, suggested by the teacher's own love for and mastery of his science. When, in my eagerness to put my interest to some good use, I asked, "What can I do?" he proposed bird-banding. He also provided me with the necessary credentials to acquire the licence.

My bird-banding station was at that time the most northerly in Ontario. It became a matter of absorbing interest to discover the patterns of birdlife, the behaviour and movements of birds in my environment in that broad zone where the north and the south meet, where the harsh nature of the Canadian Shield, full of rocks, lakes, rivers, coniferous forests and splendid beauty, grades into the gentler, more southerly, deciduous forest belt. What species were to be found here? What were the dynamics of populations and relationships, seasonal changes, nestings? And, last but not least, to have banded returning birds, or when found and caught elsewhere to learn the facts about their travels, gave promise of exciting research.

Soon I came into contact with other banders to exchange information. On a package of pamphlets received with a request to send them on to the next address, I found some scribbled remarks, very clever and amusing, with a greeting from the sender, Ralph DeLury. The name told me nothing in particular, but the note intrigued me, so I wrote a few words in reply.

It was not until later when, together with some other notes, he sent me a reprint of an article entitled "Sunspot Influences" that I realized his eminence as an astronomer. In the course of many questions asked and elementary explanations given with wonderful patience and aptness, and many discussions held without trace of arrogance from the pinnacle of his learning, my horizons widened considerably. It brought about an awareness that grew apace, starting with Sitka spruces and seeds buried in ice thousands of years ago, into an almost endless past and an infinite future, of worlds existing at unimaginable distances, all tied together. Most important of all, under DeLury's tutorship I was imbued with a strong sense of the absolute interrelationship and interdependency of all this and the miniature world in which we exist, without which, I believe, a realistic understanding of our own and the worlds beyond is hardly possible.

What, being an astronomer gazing into space, were his beliefs? In answer to my question he wrote, "All is ephemeral!" When I told him about the Old Pine, the largest and the oldest tree in the area around Pimisi Bay, with its trunk measuring about 14 feet in circumference, he became keenly interested. He judged it to be over 300 years old. I realized, surprised, that it would have stood there by the rapids of the Mattawa River when Champlain passed that exact spot with his voyageurs on his inland journey of discovery. DeLury regretted he could not get a cross-section of that trunk – he could have extracted much interesting information from it. When told of the ancient tree's demise in a wild storm, he wrote, "A southwest wind, wasn't it, that brought it down?" And he was right.

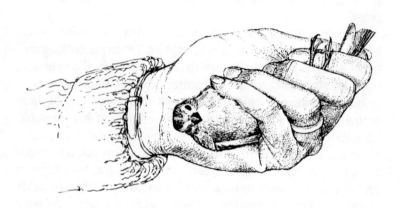

A Bird in the Hand

Bird-banding brings to the bander a dual satisfaction: the sense of contributing in at least a small way to the general store of knowledge concerning birds, and the more personal satisfaction of watching the birds daily at close range.

My banding station is in the heart of the breeding grounds for the majority of the Eastern North-American song-birds. Except for a few, such as the tree sparrow and the white-crowned sparrow which breed in the Barrens, most of their migratory flyways come to an end in this Canadian zone. My traps stand in the midst of the woods surrounding my house, their locations carefully chosen according to season and the species expected to be visiting them.

The first bird I catch, this winter of 1942, is a blue jay, a resplendent fellow which has evidently never before seen a trap. It hops into it without hesitation – to its immense

4

discomfiture. Although the bird remains in the neighbourhood for nearly three months, together with its companion which I banded soon after, they are the only blue jays to visit my feeding-station that winter. Wise birds, learning from experience and never, never forgetting, they proceed to feed from the traps in such a way as never to risk recapture. Boldly hopping up to the trap, they single out a piece of food, rush in, grasp it, duck and are off, the most expert evasive action I have ever witnessed.

Later on towards the spring, when food supplies elsewhere become temporarily scarcer, other blue jays join the first ones. Somehow the latter must have warned the newcomers about the traps. None of them, probably, had ever seen such a contraption before, yet they behave as if they know exactly what to expect. The fact that a few of them do get caught I like to attribute to their ineptitude at the evasive game rather than to ignorance.

The blue jay is a handful of blue-grey splendour. In a moment of sentimental effusion I bent over an especially handsome one in my hand and received, in return, a caress that was anything but gentle. It left a mark on my lip for a week.

The black-capped chickadee is the imp of the woods, present at the banding station throughout the winter months. It treats snow, bone-chilling frosts and traps with equal indifference. All that preoccupies it is to fill its crop with every morsel of food available. Catch it and band it, for all it cares. Back it comes into the trap the very next minute.

The first chickadee I banded was Peet. Our association dated back at least to another winter before that when, with trustful intimacy, he first took a sunflower seed from my hand. Awkwardly I turned the tiny bird over on its back into banding position, fearful lest my clumsy hand hurt it. Four years later, Peet is no longer a young bird, yet he still roams the forest, hale and hearty.

There are several hairy woodpeckers among the winter residents. Beef suet is their great weakness and, traps or no traps, they indulge their appetites often and energetically. They protest vociferously when taken from a trap. But this is only a show, for soon they are back again, peeping from behind a tree-trunk, chipping loudly. Without looking at the leg to see if the bird is banded, it is easy to tell a newcomer from a regular, for the latter approaches the trap like an old customer a familiar haunt.

With the milder winds of spring the migratory birds return. Only snow and chilly weather tempt these travellers into my traps. The ground-feeding sparrows are, as a rule, the easiest to capture. But once they are on their breeding grounds they require camouflaged traps in good positions near convenient cover. The tree sparrows are exceedingly finical in such matters and, although they may be passing through in considerable numbers, my list of banded ones is never very long.

When the first dark-eyed juncos arrive, they hop lightly across the trapping grounds, fastidiously avoiding anything that looks like a trap. But as their numbers increase into overwhelming multitudes, they consume the seeds fallen upon the snow since the fall in such quantities that the bait in the traps becomes the only alternative left to them for food. Then persuasion on my part may be abandoned, for they make feeding in the traps a habit that lasts throughout the spring season.

Another sparrow, the white-crowned, uses another approach. Its migratory passage may be somewhat erratically plotted from one year to the next, so that I cannot always count on its appearance. When they come, their visit never extends beyond two weeks – they have a long way to go to their breeding grounds in the far north. With their conspicuous white-striped crowns and dove-grey fronts, they are the most elegant of sparrows. Will such a splendid-looking bird hesitate before a trap? Never! As I trip it shut, instant panic grips the prisoner seeking frantically to find the exit. The next moment it lies in my hand limp, having given up all struggle. And I have time to admire the lustre of those brown eyes as they look into mine as if pleading this will not be its end.

The song sparrow was the first of my banded migrants to return in the spring after a winter's absence and it has always occupied a special place in my heart. I share with all banders the thrill of holding in the hand once again a bird which has travelled many hundreds of miles since I saw it last. It has found its way back to the exact spot in this wide land of the north where last year it mated and nested. What energy to be generated by so slight a body! What a wonderful instinct guides it to perform this feat of migrating seasonally from the north to the south and back!

The sparrow is easy to take this morning, for it is cold and much snow still lies on the ground. Later, he and his mate use one favourite (shall we call it that?) trap as their preferred feeding spot morning and night. With a light swoop over the stone wall he hops into the trap, chirping. She follows. And there they sit side by side, scratching a bit with both feet at once, picking, then scratching again. I put a band on her too. But the next spring the male sparrow turns up with a new mate – why, I never found out, of course.

There follows a period when neither bird is seen until the time their first brood leaves the nest. Then the male returns to the feeding-station to snatch pieces of bread. These he mashes in his bill, then carries away to feed to his young ones hidden in the underbrush. At this time he is almost impossible to trap. With a vigilance and skill common to many wild creatures during their periods of reproduction, he protects himself from danger. Uncannily alert, he senses any move I make from behind my screened window to pull the trap string, and he is out and away before I have time to blink.

This sequence of behaviour is repeated during the second breeding cycle, so that even if I never find the nest, by observing his visits at the traps I can follow the course of events pretty accurately. After the post-nuptial moult is over, the song sparrow reappears regularly and his general behaviour lapses into the casual ways of the early spring. In late October, or early November, depending on the weather, he and the junco depart, the last song-birds to leave the Pimisi Bay area in the fall.

Strange as it seems, my first acquaintance with the bronzed grackle, this ubiquitous and harsh-voiced blackbird, is auspicious – for the bird. The iridescence of its black plumage as it steps out of the shadow into a blazing ray of sunshine is a striking play of colours shivering upon its shiny black feathers. The bird is also endowed with an intelligence above the avian average. It is a devoted parent in its own nest, but accused of being an inveterate robber of other birds' nests. Of this I have no proof; I have yet to find evidence of its acting according to reputation. Circumstances here are perhaps sufficiently different from elsewhere. The abundance of natural foods, for one thing, the wild state of this country largely unaffected by civilization and its impact, the comparatively well-balanced proportion of their populations, may be sufficient to counteract the grackle's predatory inclinations.*

Whatever may be the case, I learned to appreciate the grackle, its gawky ways and squawky noises notwithstanding. With a knowing look in its straw-coloured eye, it goose-steps up and down among the traps. Whether or not it has known them from earlier experience, those wire-netted contraptions inspire it with distrust. Should the bird fare so badly as to become entrapped in one with all exits shut, this happens, not because the wretched trap surprised it, but because the bird's greed betrayed it.

When the grackle arrives upon the scene with a young one in tow, the conflict between the bird's prudence and its parental urge to feed the offspring is interesting to watch. After long hesitation and uncountable trial runs, with inimitable expertise lately acquired, the parent dashes under the trap, grasps the selected tidbit and dashes out again. The

---

*A decade later, however, the bronzed grackle, together with other blackbirds, notably the parasitic brown-headed cowbird, increased in numbers to the extent that they became a threat to other birds on these breeding grounds, and to the woodland song-birds in particular. Civilization's influence upon the environment often has far-reaching consequences. Without the slightest encouragement, the grackles gradually overran the choice nesting places, especially in the lush neighbourhoods of beaver lakes and other marshy places; spots provided with water, cover and good food supplies. Where the thrushes before intoned their delicious dawn and vesper songs, now the raucous vocalizations of the grackles replace them. Furthermore, in a population explosion of disastrous magnitude, other blackbirds and the starlings also began to invade these premises in spring and fall. Sometimes, in the name of perhaps rather ambivalent ideas of conservation, drastic action has been undertaken in vulnerable areas to check overflow assemblies of blackbirds.

immediate reaction of the fledgling is one of eager acceptance. But later, out of sight of its parent, it performs an amateur imitation act at the trap, which in nine cases out of 10 lands it in captivity. Caught, the young thing screams for help, unashamed but frantic, bites, struggles, squeals until it is released unhurt to rejoin its father, the small badge of identification securely clasped around its leg.

From a bander's viewpoint snowstorms in May are wonderful occasions for watching the entire population of transient and returned migrants emerge from cover. With their food supply buried under the snow they are starving. Once on their habitual breeding grounds the insectivorous birds ordinarily scorn the artificial offering, be it ever so tempting. But now they are driven by dire need. Elusive as ghosts, the hermit thrushes come out into the open. In a series of running hops interrupted by pauses for observation, they traverse the trap yard. Should the path take one of them into a trap, what odds! With resigned abandon, it pays for the attempted mealworm theft. Beautiful with its reddish tail and the delicate olive-brown colouring, the bird's large fawnlike eyes express the pure innocence of the untamed.

As soon as the weather improves, the birds drop back again into the undergrowth, out of sight. Catching them during the nesting season is not so easy and involves finding the nests and watching them carefully until the nestlings are about seven days old, the safe time for banding them. Using the banded nestlings as bait to capture the parents requires cautious handling. To disrupt or to destroy their nest life by clumsy interference would be to defeat the purpose of the research. The nestlings are placed in a small box close to the nest where the parents can find them and feed them either inside a trap or strategically near one. And the operation should not be unduly prolonged. Although it is estimated that only 50% of all banded fledglings survive their first year, some of the most interesting data concerning population variations, nesting success and genealogy are obtained in this way.

When the nesting season and the post-nuptial moult are over, the thrushes begin to move away from their territories in preparation for the migration. Again, they become less secretive and cautious. With the insectlife on the wane, they look for fruit as their principal sustenance. They find the blueberries of the Virginia creeper especially palatable. With a cluster of these tied inside the trap, thrush after thrush of whatever species may be passing hops into captivity without counting the cost. Time and again they "repeat" until every berry is eaten and they move on in search of other fields of plenty.

The purple finch and the evening grosbeak, the latter having not so long ago spread from the west across the east to the sea, are also among the song-birds of this forest. During certain periods of their yearly cycle they develop a peculiar taste for salt, a need that seems to reach a climax just before and during the breeding season. The reason for this is not well understood. The taste may be akin to the desire of some mammals for salt, especially during the lactation period. The finches' love for salt simplifies their capture considerably. All they need is ground well soaked with salty water and it is surprising how they discover it. Once found, on roadways or elsewhere, flock upon flock of salt-loving finches leave their nests, eggs and young, and fly marked distances to alight for a few minutes at the spot to pick the salted grit. The bander has only to set up his traps. For so long as a grain of salt remains in the ground, the birds will return, sometimes year after year, to the same place.

The salt-lick becomes a valuable indicator of population changes. One spring I banded some 30 purple finches, not nearly all that came, and only one of these "repeated." Another year in the same way I banded 30 evening grosbeaks. Had I only had enough traps and enough time I could have taken 10 times as many, for it was a peak year for evening grosbeaks in this region.

Banding large numbers of birds of one species provides an excellent opportunity to study individual variations in plumages relating to differences in age and sex. In this respect both the purple finch and the evening grosbeak are interesting subjects. In the first, the full purple plumage of the males requires several years to develop, whereas the colour patterns of the evening grosbeak show wide variations. A famous American bird-bander, M. J. Magee of Sault Ste. Marie,

Michigan, has done remarkable work on the plumage of these two species.

It is true that a bird in the hand is better than 10 in the bush. As I hold a fully matured rose-breasted grosbeak in my hand, only then do I realize he has not his equal among the woodland song-birds of our northern latitudes. No wonder Audubon found no rest until he had seen this bird in full courtship display. What exquisite joy it must have been for this talented artist to let his brush run riot through the intricate patterns of black and white, the soft seal-brown of the tail and wing quills, the red splashed down the white breast to repeat itself in the luxuriant red lining of the wings.

One day, by the merest chance, I catch in my largest trap a male ruby-throated hummingbird. For 10 unforgettable minutes this diminutive masterpiece of nature lies in the hollow of my hand. And, having beheld these two, I have seen the eight wonders of the world.

My banding activities covered a period of 17 years from 1942 to 1959. At first I used drop traps, easily manufactured of wire mesh about 36′ by 36′ with low sides, propped open on a short stick. A long string attached to the stick was pulled and the thing dropped down upon the unsuspecting bird. There were no accidents. In winter, the other end of the string was passed through tiny holes bored in the walls of the kitchen, where most of the watching, pulling and banding took place. Later I acquired a variety of automatic traps, a many-celled one to catch the ground-feeding birds, and a suspended one, the favourite of the chickadees. Some of the juncos got caught in this last one, after they learned from the chickadees there was food in them, a type of behaviour the ethologists call sympathetic induction. And finally there was one attached to the trunks of the trees, which the nuthatches, creepers and woodpeckers entered from the bottom and tripped shut on the way up to sample the suet bait. The now popular Japanese mist nets, which, with their versatile capacity of catching birds in flight, now replace most mechanized traps, were not then in vogue.

My list comprised a total of 2,628 birds banded from 50 species. Of these many returned year after year until their deaths, most often to exactly the same spot in the vast forest where they had nested the previous year. Later, after I began marking them with coloured bands, I needed only to check the position of the bands and the colour to know each bird personally and much of its history.

Of my banded birds only eight were recovered elsewhere, three of them evening grosbeaks. The most interesting of these was a male which in the course of its remaining lifetime of seven years was checked twice, once at Lebanon, New Hampshire, before it was eventually found dead at Sorel, Quebec.

In 1948, a pair of merlins, also called pigeon hawks, of the falcon family, nested in a tall white pine perched on the side of a knoll at the south end of Pimisi Bay. For three years I watched these birds return each spring to this nest to raise a family. In spectacular flights up and down the lake they taught their young ones by their example to fly, to slip and stoop, and to catch their own prey. But in the midst of their third summer the parents disappeared. Knowing the still downy nestlings would surely die if left, I brought them down and two of them happily survived on dog meat and raw liver. They learned to fly by themselves and in time stooped expertly to grasp the pieces of liver laid out for them. On September 3 they migrated together. A year later one of them was recovered dead at Eagle's Nest Resort in Stasca County, Minnesota, no less than 1,000 miles due west of its birthplace. The fate of the other one was never known.

Identification of individual birds opened a wide range of new possibilities. No longer was there any guesswork. Now I could follow the birds' territorial and sexual relationships with assurance. Suddenly caught in the focus of my binoculars, the bright-coloured male yellow-rumped warbler high up in the top of the aspen revealed a red band on its right leg. It could be none other than the bird I had held in my hand last spring, when it arrived in a snowstorm and was caught in the suet-baited trap.

Soon I found that his behaviour also tallied well with his status as a returned migrant. First of the species to be seen, he conformed with the quite common habit of birds returning, earlier than the rest, to the area where they had lived before. And by flying around and singing loudly from certain perches, he also immediately claimed the same territory which, with only minor variations, he had occupied last year.

It is fascinating to follow the pairing and the mating of individually known birds. They can spring many surprises upon the observer. Conjugal faithfulness in natural surroundings, free from artificial pressures, is also of great interest. Polygyny, polygamy, even extra-marital relationships, all exist and always in connection with some logical circumstance of one kind or another to influence it, such as population balances, the scarcity or abundance of food. What happens when liaisons are broken by death? How do widowed mates react?

One may penetrate into parental behaviour. There are many variations, individual and specific, personal recognition, and many other aspects, some surprisingly analogous to human behaviour. On this subject Konrad Lorenz, the Nobel-prize winner, has probably contributed the most brilliant analyses.

In the end there is age. How long does a bird live, what is its life expectancy? The smaller the bird, the shorter its life. Yet I know, and several others have also established the fact, that a chickadee may live to be nine years old, a considerable age for such a fast-metabolizing small bird. One grey jay, a larger bird, was 10 years old when it disappeared, and a female hairy woodpecker, the larger of the two most common woodpeckers in our forest, was carefully monitored from month to month until she reached the age of 17 years in the spring of 1970, less one or two weeks. She was banded October 9, 1953, almost surely in her first year of life.

Winter Birds at the Loghouse

In the fall of 1947 a blissful Indian summer lasted for weeks instead of a few short days. Night after night *aurora borealis* wafted long undulating sheets of heavenly illumination across the skies, sometimes with the faintest tints of pink and green. In the forests around Pimisi Bay, every balsam, spruce, and tamarack, every pine and cedar tree, stood weighted down with enormous clusters of cones in such abundance as I have never seen. It seemed to me an exciting possibility that these circumstances, in combination with the fruitful cones, gave promise of something unusual in the way of winter birds.

It began with the red-breasted nuthatches and the brown creepers. In other years only an occasional one of these birds stayed to pass the winter in this 46th latitude. But this time eight nuthatches and four brown creepers lingered on through those balmy days of autumn. When the black-capped chickadees, with their elfin fuss and chatter, attracted the nuthatches and the creepers to the suet and the peanut butter offered at my window, they abandoned all further urge to move on and remained to face whatever might be in store for them.

On November 24, small flocks of evening grosbeaks, which had been rare all summer, kept coming in from the north in the early mornings. Sometimes they would put the brakes on their swooping flight and with a ringing call come down, handsome and proud, to smudge their light-coloured bills in the salty gravel of the highways. With them there were at times small groups of purple finches, mostly young ones with a faint rosy tint over their drab immature plumages. They said *tuck-tuck*, pecked the salt and ate the buds of the poplars, birches, and alder bushes in their spare time. I wondered why they had not gone south long ago.

On November 24, I ran into a huge flock of snow buntings. In the hundreds they lifted and swarmed around me and the car, harmlessly glancing off the hood as we slid to a stop in the midst of this multitude of white wings. With their trilling notes they whirled around us in dancing disorder, and then drifted out over the fields like so many large feather-light snowflakes.

That night – a fairy night – the woods were dusted with the first snowfall, a woolly layer of fresh snow that left them standing virginal and pure in the moon's silvery sheen. Dawned the first crystal-crisp winter's morning. The lake covered itself with thin detached sheets of ice that eventually spread out over a few black runners of still open water. I knew then that winter was upon us. With the ice and snow taking command of land and water, the feeding place at the house became the rendezvous of the winter birds. As a stop-sign for any northern finches, crossbills, pine grosbeaks and others that might happen along, I kept a place clear of snow and made it look attractively brown and bare with coal ashes. On this I placed a block of rock salt, knowing the finches' taste for salt. As it melted, it deposited delectable crystals on the surrounding snow and ashes, but it took the birds some time to discover it.

Red-breasted nuthatches, those engaging small, slate-blue birds with their bills cheekily upturned and their tails too short, came to the feeding-station. The first one that took the daring flight to the suet in the window was a female. As she flew into the cherry tree, she saw a chickadee feeding at the window. She stopped short, upside down, with her bill turned up higher than ever. Curiosity soon got the better of her and she came over. She said *tetetetetet*, fluttered her wings, apparently addressing an unseen male, took a piece of suet and flew away with it. The next instant, a male appeared, took a sunflower seed and flew off. But he did not know what to do with it, so he dropped it. He returned, said *yank-yank-yank* through his nose, and attacked the suet. And so it began.

The first nuthatch I banded hissed at me. It was a big hiss for so small a bird. For a time hissing became the nuthatches' main way of asserting themselves around the feeding place. Dramatic encounters ensued between them and the well-established chickadees. The intrepid small strangers rose to their toes in pygmy ire, advanced upon the black-cap with wings opened, like owls do in defence, but which in the nuthatch became an act in miniature, ridiculous to witness. In the face of this, the chickadee sat back and gave a high-pitched trill and then hastily retreated before a mock chase by the hissing nuthatch. Later on, habit and hunger inspired both species with a more tolerant and companionable spirit.

Once a strange nuthatch appeared upon the scene. He was greeted by loud *yank*ing from all the home birds, which hopped about in great excitement, wings drooped and tails in the air. Now and again they batted their wings and drove home their point with a stuttering string of *tututututut* or *titititit*. But the undaunted newcomer returned stare for stare. This exhibition went on for 12 minutes, after which the desire for food got the better of all of them.

As to the creepers, they became very interested in the peanut butter smeared on the trunk of a red pine. There they sat, fluffed up for comfort in the below-zero weather with their chestnut rumps showing and pecking delicately with their fine curved bills. Once in a while they called to each other with their faint long trill. Or if I disturbed them, they gave a fine reproachful *tzi tzi* and flew away to another trunk. When all the peanut butter was eaten, they sometimes descended to a banding trap to look for a piece of suet. No matter if the trap was not set, the creepers blissfully caught themselves anyway by forgetting entirely which way they came in.

Two middle-aged female hairy woodpeckers returned to spend the winter in the vicinity of the feeding place they knew so well. They staggered their visits to the suet. In the course of time a young female discovered the creepers' peanut butter in the red pine. The creepers did not mind sharing it with anybody. But the two old woodpeckers launched an immediate protest against this immature invasion. By turns they chased the young female until one of them finally cornered her in a dead poplar. There the two sat with spread tails, the young one clinging to the under-side of the branch and the old one above. Between periods of frozen immobility they opposed each other in a standing dance of bizarre gestures, flapping their wings in unison and thrusting their heads from side to side. The young one refused to be intimidated. After that, all three birds staggered their visits to the feeding place.

A black-backed three-toed woodpecker, which in the summer had discovered two dying red pines at the house, kept up regular periodic visits to these trees. She was a bird of shining black without the orange patch which adorns the male's crown. Her finely barred flank feathers in black and white stood about her like a soft fuzzy fringe. When alarmed, she uttered a sharp *chick* very like the cardinal's alarm note. Usually she arrived early in the morning. It took her several hours to go over the trunks of the pines from roots to crowns to locate the existent tidbits. With deft powerful blows of her bill she peeled off pieces of bark, then licked up the larvae that were killing the trees. When she left, the place was strewn with debris, in which the creepers crept about happily, having a festive snack.

Early in December I got the first inkling that the highlight of this winter season was about to develop. I saw flocks of purple finches, pine siskins and winter-dressed goldfinches. Long ago they should have disappeared from the wintry north.

I first met the birds on the highways. In flocks of various sizes they intermixed with small numbers of red crossbills and the evening grosbeaks, which stood high in the pecking order. Only the redpolls, ordinarily the most common among the winter birds from the far north, stayed away until February, when a few of them appeared with their red caps drawn down over their crowns.

The birds sat, engrossed in pecking salty gravel with which the roads had been sanded during the winter. Scores of them were killed by passing cars. Even the careful motorist had difficulty avoiding them, for they sat so tight, lifting only at the last split second. One day I picked up four white-winged crossbills just killed by a passing car, and I regretted intensely that the dead bodies of these beautiful birds in my hand should be my first introduction to this interesting species. The next thing I knew, I found that the woods were full of them.

One day the finches discovered my feeding-station under the pines. Never before had the small place in front of my window seen such moving twittering multitudes of birds. I could not even count them as they flew off and returned, whirled and swirled with a chorus of finchy notes. They relished the crystals of the rock salt and crowded around snow patches discoloured by slop water, avoiding my three banding traps set in this narrow space, disdaining every kind of seed I offered as bait. My banding records show little evidence of the abundance of these birds. Even the two purple finches I eventually caught, birds that in the summer are easily lured into my traps with millet and hemp, were now caught on 20% salted coal ashes and 80% good luck.

Soon I found what attracted these high-flying birds to our woods. They came for the evergreen seeds in the cones, and because of these they remained. The hard brown seeds under the husks of the cones indeed possessed the highly nutritive ingredients which not only reconditioned the birds for their coming nesting season, but also enabled them to withstand the cold of this latitude, where the temperatures may well fall to

40° below zero. Neither heavy snowfalls nor several feet of snow covering the ground was of any account to them, when every tree in the forest was the storage room of plenty, capable of supporting hundreds of birds throughout the winter.

The balsam firs' small upright cones were the first to be emptied. The opening cones of the trees shed the ripe seeds and the nuthatches quickly discovered the bounty. Soon for miles around all that remained of the firs' rich cone harvest were the bare stems looking like stripped bobbins. And the snow below was littered with the husks.

When this food was devoured, I expected the finches to leave for better feeding grounds. But instead they attacked the cones of the white spruces and the white and red pines, which they pilfered without removing the husks. The tamarack cones found favour with the purple finches and the white-winged crossbills, and the small conelike seed stores of the alder bushes with the pine siskins. Even if I did not see them, I always knew of the passing visit of a flock of evening grosbeaks or pine grosbeaks by the remainders of their hearty meal of winged seed containers scattered on the snow below the mountain maple bushes.

Rare birds are always the object of the bird watcher's special interest. Their stories are so full of unwritten pages. With the attractive crossbills, unpredictable and unbound by any season as their appearances and nestings are, their appeal is strong for additional reasons.

They are undoubtedly two of the most beautiful species of the northern finches. The individual variations in their plumages are so great that, especially in the red crossbill, I can hardly recall having seen two birds exactly alike. The basic colour of the female is greenish-grey and of the male, yellowish-red with dark brown wings and tail. A varying amount of yellowish-bronze, particularly on the crown and breast, increasing in brightness on the rump, distinguishes many of the females from each other. The juvenile male is like the female, but from his first year to adulthood he apparently goes through as many changes as he has moults, in which the greenish-grey and yellowish-red colours battle for predominance.

In the white-wing the black wings with the "pearly" design of their two bars and the white edging of the tertial wing feathers are striking features which lend a butterfly appearance to the birds in flight. The female is olive-green, darkly striped on the back, with a varying degree of yellow-bronze and a bright yellow rump. From the first sight of the fully mature male, I decided that, in him, the rose-breasted grosbeak had its equal.

The flight of the crossbills is swooping and airy. Incredibly long glides with wings tight against the body are relieved by a few beats of the wings, giving the birds either a new soaring lift or, with an abrupt twist of acrobatic agility, a change of direction.

Long before the birds are in sight they announce themselves by clear whistled call-notes, *peet-wheet-wheet*, given as often in flight as perched in a tree-top. The white-wing's song is like that of a slightly muted canary's. Their notes are softer, sweeter, more musical than the red crossbill's, whose call sometimes comes almost as loudly as the pine grosbeak's and with a metallic resonance. And even though I have often heard the crossbills singing, without the evidence of the eye I am loath to decide which one the singer is, perched high in the top of the pine, whose notes drop so deliciously upon the hoarfrosty air. The song of the red crossbill is like the music of water and that of the white-wing like an enchanted music box, which cannot stop until entirely run down.

A coincidental element certainly belonged to this unusual invasion of cone-seed eating finches. At that time these regions were still thinly populated and man's impact upon the natural environment was negligible. The land, remaining largely untouched, was rich in wildlife, the numbers of which were subject mainly to the natural balances. It so happened that in this year seven of the species of conifers in this eastern forest, the white cedar or *arbor vitae*, the red and white pines, the black and white spruces, the balsam firs and the tamaracks, all producing cone growth with cyclic regularity, stood laden with a bumper crop of cones at the same time. When the seed-eating finches during their fall and winter travels found this abundant source of food, they came in greater and greater

numbers, guided into the region of plenty by whatever pressures might have urged them. As salt is a digestive need for certain mammals living on a vegetable diet, such as the porcupine subsisting on poplar bark in winter, the deer eating cedar boughs, so also salt is a need connected with the consumption of quantities of evergreen seeds. And it was the salt that brought the finches to the feeding-station.

They began to roost in the tops of the pines surrounding the house. As light seeped in almost like liquid over the land and flooded the tops of the trees, continuous warbled notes poured softly from the invisible birds. From the crossbills in that tree, the pine siskins in this one, and the goldfinches in the next one, all unseen, the enchanting matutinal concert filled the crisp air until the light grew strong and the birds almost on one accord flew out. This was the first sign. As winter's end approached there were still seeds aplenty in the cones. To birds like these of nomadic habits food and breeding belong together and the start of the nesting cycle is often adjusted accordingly.

In a small area atop the tall cliffs above the river, I found four nests of the red crossbills, distributed among the feathery spruces. Before the snows melted and while the ice was still thick on the lakes and the rivers, these nests contained eggs, from which full clutches hatched. Near and far the parents foraged, filling their crops with seeds, and then pouring this half-digested porridge down the hungry gapes of the young ones. And they grew and prospered.

In a bog where the black spruces, slender of growth and dark green, crowded together with their roots deep in the swampy soil, where the naked tamaracks bore rows of tight brown cones on short curved stalks along their horizontal branches, some of which had opened like small brown roses, I found pair upon pair of white-winged crossbills. They were engaged in elaborate courtship ceremonies, singing, nest-building and egg-laying. All over the forest male pine siskins, their tails and wing-flashes shining faintly yellow or white in the warming sun, rapturously enacted in circles over the tree-tops their possessive flight songs, while somewhere in the thickest branches of an evergreen their mates were busily constructing their well-padded moss nests.

Never again during the next 30 years was there to be a similar coincidence capable of bringing together in this region so many finches with such a plentiful source of their favourite food. At long intervals during these years I was to see only odd pairs of red crossbills in some secluded spot, cryptic enough in their demeanour to suggest a hidden nest. Or a small flock of pine siskins coming out of nowhere to settle for a short stay in the neighbourhood of the feeding-station, there to pilfer something that looked like the same stuff they were looking for – and then go on. And I might snowshoe into the thick stands of black spruces of the bog in the deep snow of a late winter day, possessed of a nostalgic desire to see if, perchance, a pair or two of white-wings might not have returned to break the heavy silence with a series of their canary-like trills and warbles. But there were none.

Bird feeding-stations have nowadays become a common

accessory, almost a passion with ordinary people as well as with bird-watchers. Apart from the joy and the excitement of watching these ethereal creatures at close range to marvel at the shape, the balance of the feather-light body, the use of the tail, a wing in flight or to discover what kind of birds are around, feeding-stations are established with a feeling that birds could not do without them. This is conservation. Elaborate devices are worked out to attract the birds. Feeders are constructed with both aesthetic and practical purposes in mind: self-serve boxes and jars, suet logs pleasing to the human eye principally, shelter-type shelves that protectingly swing with the wind. Seed mixes and other prepared foods are sold to suit not only the needs but also the habits and tastes of the various kinds of birds. And the question arises: Of what actual merit is a bird feeding-station?

Had I been asked this question at the time when the events just described took place, I would with great enthusiasm have launched into a lively discussion on the indispensability of the feeding-station. With experience certain doubts have arisen.

Although there are many ways of studying birds and their habits and their behaviour, for the keen bird-watcher and the serious ornithological student the feeding-station has distinct merit. It is a legitimate and conservation-oriented enterprise.

However, it should not be forgotten that, even if located in a natural setting, the feeding-station is not a natural asset but a contrived artificiality that affects the environment as well as the birds themselves, causing sometimes anomalous reactions.

A bird passing by finds the feeding-station. Its companions take note. The ample easily picked food appeals and tempts them to return. Gradually others are attracted by their example. Too many birds assembling within a limited space tend to become noisy. Competition interjects tension. Movement is increased. This, in turn, attracts birds that prey on birds. And while this also has the effect of increasing the birds' vigilance to ever-present dangers, it also fosters exaggerated excitability. The birds' wild headlong dash to escape the danger in an unnatural environment filled with see-through glass sometimes kills as surely as the predator's claw.

The birds do not in general need the food offered at the

feeding-station. This is especially true during the seasons when the natural environment contains rich amounts of insectlife, fruits and seeds. The wild bird's principal occupations are movement and food finding. Its schedule closely follows the diurnal circumstances and contributes significantly to the natural balances of its environment. There is space, there is search, there is the well-balanced impact of the bird's activities upon the world surrounding it. Food too easily found tends to disorganize this schedule and inhibits the element of search in its behaviour. The filled feeder replaces not only the natural food but also the diversity of the items found by the searching bird.

In many places along the great migration routes the too-generous feeding of the migrating wildfowl has over the years caused problems, such as local overcrowding and various kinds of destruction. It has also made wild birds tame and dependent on the artificial food sources. Wildness, the wild creature's most vital asset of self-preservation, is lost. Lost is the daring, the spark that fires the successful escape, blunted is the instinct to avoid the too-close approach of a stranger. The migratory urge to disperse into the normal spacious, more varied, wintering grounds is weakened. The equilibrium between the populations of living creatures and the environment, constantly being corrected in a multitude of ways, is thoughtlessly being sacrificed to the detriment of both the birds and the environment.

In our efforts to achieve some meaningful success in conservation, to act or not to act has become – with the spread of humanity and the changing environment – most difficult to decide. Interference, of whatever kind, might well be likened to a double-edged sword. The feeding-station, therefore, as a minor part of the conservation effort, and if it is to be of environmental value, needs judicious and knowledgeable management. For the bird, once conditioned to the free offerings, will return again and again – and again.

Part Two

First Insights

If you really want to know a bird, find its nest! For the keen and alert observer, I will guarantee much excitement and startling surprises.

Sit by the nest! Forget that you yourself exist, but throw all your attention upon the bird that you are watching! For it is volatile. It is full of individualism. Like you, it is buffeted by impressions and is the plaything of circumstances. It acts by instinct, some prescribed by set patterns, some fastened by stereotyped releasers that take no note of subtle changes or differences.

Whatever you grasp of its movements and actions well enough to understand the meaning, you must absorb, not from your own standpoint but from that of the bird, your object of study. The bird's impulses are vastly different from yours – not necessarily lesser in a scale of values, but different. The level of development, experience, life-style, all play significant roles.

Emotions – yes, certainly, the most primitive: anger, fear, timidity, aggression, submissiveness, but not reasoning. This is the difference. The most difficult as well as the most interesting part lies in the fact that the human being and the bird share certain stages of behavioural development, although in different measure. But, with certain limitations, one can learn to understand from movements and actions what moods are likely to possess the bird at certain times or in given situations.

You will find the study enthralling. Not at first, perhaps, because you know so little. You misinterpret much of what you see, because the temptation to let your own feelings become involved is so great, inevitably, I would say, until you learn to check the inclination to liken the bird to yourself.

But the bird is different. From this difference emerges the qualities that make it into the creature it is, not like anything else, yet related, however distantly, in the unique way that everything upon this earth and, indeed, in the whole of the universe is related and a part.

All nests are different, all birds are different one from the other. Respect the difference! But penetrate into its essentials – and you shall know. Every detail is important and meaningful. You must note and record meticulously every detail, every happening of which you become aware. Very gradually, very slowly, you will realize the meaning of a given gesture, a circumstance, the way a leaf hangs, the manner in which a strand of cobweb trails from its original position, the way two birds meet, the way a bird flies, twitters, sings, picks its food, eats, scratches, moves. All of this underlines a mood, an urge, sets off a sequence attached to the past and flowing into the future. Take it all down! Every minute detail is significant. As you observe, you will see more. As you absorb the interrelated connections, you will understand better the vast possibilities of reaction involved in the bird's life.

There are open nests, there are nests built or bored into holes, burrows and recesses, and some birds make no nests at all. The open nests of the perching birds are most exposed, most difficult to protect from the constant dangers that assail them. Some protection exists, good cover and the surreptitious comings and goings of the parent birds. But necessary parental absences cause sometimes large open holes, as it were, in the protective canopy of vigilance that normally surrounds the exposed nest. So let the nestlings flee the nest quickly! And most of them do in 8, 10, 12 days, to exchange one danger-filled existence for another, free of action it is true, but still precarious to an infantile fledgling untrained in the art of split-second escapes. Once outside the nest, the training proceeds apace. Each day of life won is to the young bird another day's chance of survival.

By comparison nests in holes are safer. Yet the elements of risk prevail in them also. This is a natural provision whereby the number of individuals of a species as well as its survival value are strictly controlled; and the provision is necessary and ultimately to the benefit of the species. Inside the cavity the young ones live and grow, sheltered from the weather and unseen by prying eyes, until their scent strikes a chance response in a passing predator. The safety of the young birds brought up in cavities still depends on the attentive guardian-ship of their parents. For while an adult bird caught outside usually is no match against a roused predator, such as a snake or a squirrel, inside, sitting in the narrow opening with all flanks protected and its sharp bill on the ready, the defender is all but invincible. (I am speaking of natural cavities, not bird-boxes.)

The nestling period in cavity-nesting birds is prolonged, not counted in days but in weeks. In due time the young emerge full-fledged, able to fly with powerful wing-beats and a good chance of survival, bar the risks commonly attached to juvenile inexperience.

Trials of a
Phoebe Family

It was not until 1947 that I found the eastern phoebe nesting near the house. Previously the bird had made only casual appearances in the early spring, passing by on its way to the falls of Talon Chute about a mile northward up the Mattawa River, where in summer one might always find this flycatcher. Once, I found a nest here tucked in upon a shelf under an overhanging rock, with nothing below but the turbulent waters of the 75-foot drop. This is a favoured spot for phoebes. It has running water with millions of flies dancing above the swirling surface; nesting ledges in the old timber sluices and runways and in the cliffs of the river gorge; and undisturbed peace at the height of the nesting and black fly season.

Then, early in April, I saw a phoebe, almost surely a young male, singing at the bridge of the causeway crossing Pimisi Bay. The next thing I knew nest-building was going on in full swing, not under the bridge as one might have expected, but at Big Hill, about 200 feet away. On a ledge, at the top of the steep sandy bank of the highway, not far from the belted kingfisher's hole, the nest had been built, roofed over by a piece of turf. This nest successfully fledged two young and soon after the family moved off to parts unknown.

The next year the same birds returned. They took up the same territory as the year before and built their nest a few feet from the old site, but this time the phoebes had the whole earth bank to themselves because the kingfisher moved across the highway to the south side. I do not know if there was any connection between the kingfisher's move and the phoebes' misfortune, but nearly two weeks after the young phoebes hatched, the nest was torn out by some four-footed creature. Only the male phoebe was seen again after this, and it is likely that both the female and the young were killed. I thought that this was the end of the phoebe story.

I think it was the widowed male phoebe that, next spring, came down from the skies into the top of a tall poplar at Big Hill one beautiful April morning. Without feeding, or any other preliminaries, he forthwith cast his notes upon the four winds, *phoebe! pheebee!* once again proclaiming his right to this piece of land, the north bank, the gully and the edge of the forest on both sides of the highway. Since the day when his first mate had led him thither from the bridge – because, to phoebes in spring, bridges and ledges, roofs and nests seemed to be closely connected – this spot had been his. It was the goal to which he had flown, the place to which, so long as he lived, he must always return.

Here all was as before. The cars rushed by over the brow of the hill and the belted kingfisher, with his blue-white plumage silvered in the sun, shot by on rhythmic wing-beats. A snowstorm followed that balmy April morning and during this period the phoebe kept himself close to the ground where the awakened insects sought refuge. In competition with many other birds and occupied with the matter of keeping alive, the phoebe had no time for singing. In such an emergency his territory lost its restricting influence over his movements and this was how he came to visit the house.

As he swung up against the wall to catch an early mosquito dancing under the eave or a spider descending its silver thread, the phoebe discovered two shelves, one under the peak of the roof at the front, the other under the eave at the back. He became vastly interested in one of these. He flew in, sat on the shelf several minutes, then flew out again. With growing excitement he flew in and out, uttering a soft whistle and a trill, *whuit-whuit-thrrrr*. He repeated the same procedure over and over again as if he could not have enough of this charming place. It was evident that his male nesting instincts were working up to a climax.

Two days later a gentle creature exactly like himself came, and she was all teetering tail and airiness. The male gave a strange quavering note, something between the soft note of the Canada jay and the alarm note of the Baltimore oriole, and his excitement suddenly knew no bounds. The female flew in on the shelf, and he came there too. She flew out; he flew out and in again with his whistle and a trill. He flew to a perch and sang and then to the shelf at the back of the house, then to the front, in and out, presenting her with all the amazing possibilities of his kingdom. By his eagerness alone she should have been easily persuaded, and she was.

For the next couple of days the pair examined shelves at the house and at the garage by the highway, 400 feet away. The little female apparently knew nothing about the steep sandy bank where the male had previously nested and his only return to the old territory was to deliver his first songs of the day from there. Early one morning there was courtship feeding on our bedroom window, a thrilling little affair full of phoebe grace and low twitterings. That afternoon the female began carrying nesting materials to a very narrow ledge above the window of an abandoned building 400 feet from the house and the garage.

She gathered mud and wet moss of the species wavy dicranum at the spring. She dropped it airily on the narrow ledge from which it promptly fell down. Undaunted, she perched on a twig, flipped her tail and said *thurrup*, as if vastly pleased with her labours. Thereupon she caught a fly and departed back to the spring. She made trip after trip and the male escorted her unfailingly. He sat on a twig as she worked, then flew to inspect the would-be nest.

How long she would have gone on with this futile work I cannot tell. After she had spent two days on it, I took pity upon her and fixed a strip of wire-mesh on the ledge for better support, but she fluttered to the ledge, dismayed at the sight of the wire, and dropped her mud and moss on the ground. She made several more fruitless trips, obviously expecting to see the ledge resume its familiar appearance. When it failed to do so, both birds flew around the building in search of another ledge. By evening they had abandoned the nesting site.

The next morning the pair were at the house again, then flew to the garage. About 9:00 a.m. the female began placing moss and mud on an artificial shelf in a corner under the eave of the garage. Towards the end of the day her little heap of material started to take the form of a nest.

It took her five days to complete the nest. This time she gathered her materials close by from rocks and tree trunks. Sometimes she made as many as three trips in four minutes. As light as air, she flitted up to the shelf and gave her purring note, *thurrup*, as if to encourage the nest as well as herself. Her shaping of the nest was done with the utmost grace, a snuggling movement, then a half-turn, then again she burrowed her breast into the nest-cup. When she finished with the moss and mud, she collected fine sticks and tendrils and frilly weeds. The male, meanwhile, sat on a twig and flipped his tail. Every so often he inspected her work and occasionally did a little shaping himself, but he never carried any material, nor was he heard to sing during this time.

Four days after the nest was finished the female laid the first egg, incubation began after she laid the fourth egg and she laid the fifth one the next morning.

All seemed serene and the phoebes' nesting place surely was the safest one in the territory. To forestall human disturbance I put a notice on the garage door bidding all visitors: *"Please pass around the corner quickly, quietly and without looking!"* Lest there be any Lot's wives among them, I added a promise to explain when they reached the house.

I discovered the first inkling of disaster when on a Sunday morning both birds came to examine the nesting shelves at the house. Again a predator had violated the phoebes' nest, had eaten three of the eggs, pierced one and left the fifth entire. I wondered if there existed a place or a situation in which the safety of a bird's nest was not a wholesale gamble with luck!

The birds took a day and a half to reach a decision about the next nesting site. Scores of times the female crouched on the shelves at the house. As the male came to show his interest she gave the quavering note. These days he spent most of his time singing.

Around noon she carried the first load of moss to the shelf at the back of the house, just above our bedroom window. At the garage she had placed the nest on the outside ledge, but this time she tucked it into the farthest and darkest corner under the eave. The male stopped singing as soon as the work on the nest began, but sang a few songs after the female finished working for the day. After that she only came and crouched in the nest as if she could not bear to be away from it too long.

With the birds so close, I discovered now that both of them roosted on the shelf, because about 4:30 the first morning, they began to twitter on the nest and six minutes later both flew out from the nesting shelf. After they fed, the female resumed work. She worked most energetically in the mornings and generally wound up the day's labours about 3:00 p.m. When the weather was too bad she did very little, merely visited the nest and crouched in it. This nest also took her five days to complete. She used the same materials in the same order as before, adding felt padding from a piece of felt that we had tied to a branch of the cherry tree. She spent a whole day with this padding, working it into the lining, and she made an accomplished job of it.

This time, after she had finished the nest, she took only a three-day holiday before she laid her first egg. Now both birds kept much closer watch over the nest and as a warning they gave abrupt ejaculations, *cheese-it*, *cheese-it*. They scolded me with a sharp *chip-chip* note and they chased away the chickadees, the hummingbird and the Blackburnian warbler.

That day the male celebrated. I had never before heard or seen the flight song of the phoebe, but as the two birds sat close together on their favourite look-out, he suddenly flung himself into the air above her with a long, loud whistled note followed by a string of rapidly uttered *phoebe*s.

That night the female roosted on the nest alone. The fourth and the fifth eggs she laid in the middle of the day, instead of the morning, and with them the female once more started to incubate.

Followed 15 days of peacefulness. Except on chilly days when she had to eat more often, the female was on the nest almost constantly. The male often perched on the open window below her for long periods of time. With head and bill raised and his tail flipping gently, he sat facing up towards her. A dragonfly pursuing its erratic course caught his attention, but it did not entice him from his perch. Once in a while he lifted his wings as if on the point of flight, but he did not forsake his mate as she sat far back in her dark corner.

I could feel the excitement that possessed the birds the day the young hatched. Their tails flipped much more vigorously and they flitted to and fro in a kind of mild aggressiveness and uttered their *cheese-it* note often. The birds never let the nest out of their sight. They divided their time between three main look-outs, the tops of a cherry tree and two dead poplars in front of the house. As the female fluttered out of the nest after a period of brooding, the male flew to meet her. He escorted her to her perch and softly batted his wings.

The mutual efforts of these two parent birds, their perseverance and patience, deserved recognition. But the greater the importance attached to an outcome the more chance appears to work against it. With each day that passed the young became older, required more attention and approached their release from the nest. To me, each day seemed a day of grace, fraught with tension. The day the red squirrel ran up on the peak of the roof and peered over the edge of the eave, and the day the garter snake chased the leopard frog into the grass under the nest, were days of painful dread for me. Had the squirrel seen or smelled the young phoebes? Could the snake climb the walls? I wanted to surround the little nest with a protective screen against the dangers of the world, but I could not. I believe that for all wild things, the natural interplay between failure and success, safety and danger, must not be eliminated lest life for them should lose its edge, and living its zest.

And so the young grew. They opened their eyes on the sixth day, gave audible food calls on the seventh and filled the nest on the thirteenth. From then on there was no longer room for the female to sit on the nest at night, so she just perched on the rim, her soft breast a shield between the night's dangers and her young.

More days passed and I asked myself: How eternally long do young phoebes remain in the nest? On the sixteenth day the youngsters stood up and stretched their legs. One surmised something was about to happen. The male sang a great deal and the parents cleared house around the nest, not even permitting two young downy woodpeckers with red frontal patches to feed as usual on the suet stick. As one behaviour cycle was coming to a close, the female was obviously passing into another. For the first time since the nest-building she examined the shelf *in front* of the house, gave her purring nest note, and that night she did not roost with her well-grown youngsters.

During the forenoon of the following day, the great event took place. One by one the young phoebes fluttered from the nesting shelf into a tangle of weeds and bush honeysuckle. Two days later the family was gone and nothing remained but an empty nest under the eave.

Red-Breast Makes a Home

The fall, winter and spring of 1947-1948 was a record year at Pimisi Bay for evergreen cones, finches and red-breasted nuthatches. In the first week of September the nuthatches had discovered the wealth of cones in the tops of the balsam firs, small and tall.

It was one day in November that a female red-breasted nuthatch came to the feeding-station. Upside down on the trunk, with her bill in the air, she watched with an interested eye as a chickadee fed at the feeders outside my window. The next moment she came over and perched bravely on the bar to which a piece of suet was attached. She quivered her wings, persuasively I thought, as if she wished to draw the attention of a bird I could not see. She gave point to her gesture by uttering a string of *te-te-te-te-te-te* notes, slow, faster, then very fast. Taking some suet, she flew off.

The next instant a fine-looking male alighted on the bar. He took a sunflower seed from the chickadees' tray and, without knowing exactly what to do with it, departed. A moment later he was back for another seed. Precisely and purposefully he did this and with a mien of knowing what he was about. This was the beginning.

The next day the male entered my banding trap quite unawares. I put a red band on his right leg, wherefore he was named Red. Shortly after, the female also entered the trap. Desperately she struggled in my hand and scolded and hissed loudly as she found herself a prisoner. Red heard her and immediately attended her. He hung from a twig above us and said, *te-te-te-te*. This, evidently, had a soothing effect on the bird in my hand, for she went limp and resigned herself to the inevitable. On one of her legs I placed a blue band. Bluey later became the "leading lady" in the development of this story.

After the first advance, it took the nuthatches no time to feel at home at the feeding place. Though as a rule not overly aggressive, the nuthatches commanded caution in the chickadees, merely by sitting back on their heels with wings and tails spread fan-wise. In vain a chickadee opened his bill in wordless self-defence, in vain he raised his crest to shoo away his opponent – the nuthatches refused to be impressed.

By this time another pair of nuthatches had invaded the feeding place and, in the course of the winter, two more pairs arrived, and a single nuthatch or two. How long these pairs had been travelling together was a matter of guessing, depending perhaps on circumstances and age. Young birds, I have learned, are more apt to wander singly until a likely partner comes along.

The close attachment between the members of a pair of nuthatches was obvious by their constant animated dialogues, their comings and goings together, and their wing-quivering when approaching close to each other, particularly on the part of the females. Furthermore, an unpaired bird, arriving, never stayed unless there happened to be an unattached member of the opposite sex around. As this was in the off-season when conjugal bonds between birds were usually dissolved, it points to the possibility that red-breasted nuthatches, like the white-breasted, remain paired throughout the year.

The arrival of a new nuthatch, especially a male, caused great perturbance among those that already considered themselves in residence. Challenging the intruder by intensive *yank*ing and defiance written all over them, they hopped along the branches posturing with wings dropped and stubby tails in the air, an eloquent way of requesting a speedy withdrawal from their midst. Undaunted, the new bird generally answered in kind. Ridiculous to behold, these demonstrations often went on from 10 to 15 minutes, before the desire for food toned down nuthatch feelings.

Thus we settled down for the winter. There was a short period when much snow and cold weather prevented these side-shows, for energies must be preserved if the birds were to survive. But even then it was evident that some spring-like instinct stirred. So, in the midst of the din and competition, members of various pairs of both sexes would alight on the birdhouse in the red cherry tree or at the edge of an old woodpecker hole, crawl around the opening and peek in, for a while wholly absorbed in its possibilities as a nesting site. Not that any of these would be considered seriously as prospective nest holes, but a cavity is inviting to a nuthatch, even in the middle of winter.

When the sun of February began to eat up the snow, intolerance between the males which were now zealously guarding their mates gave rise to prolonged chases at the feeding place where they met.

Of a sudden, a whirlwind of nuthatches whizzed madly around a tree or zigzagged in and out among bushes and trunks, accompanied by a chorus of excited *thrrrr* notes. By this time the worst of winter was over and it was no longer necessary for the nuthatches to conserve their energy to survive. One early morning in March, with a gesture of male concern as old as the ages, one of the males fed suet twice to his begging mate, for she was hungry.

It was at this time that my ear gradually became attuned to the nuthatch song. Vociferous as the nuthatch is in his stuttering way, only after a while I realized that a new long-drawn series of notes, *wewewewewewewe*, was the prolonged song of a nuthatch, as meaningful as any other bird song. It was slightly reminiscent of the junco's song, a little harsher, though neither unmusical nor lacking in emotion. Later, at other incursions of red-breasted nuthatches, I also heard the song. And it was always followed by the first meaningful sexual chase, inaugurating the courtship of the pair.

On March 29, walking high on the hard crusted snow, I stopped to listen to a faint knocking sound. To my surprise, because it was still so wintry at this latitude, I found Bluey, the female wearing my blue band, clinging to an old poplar stump, excavating a round hole 15 feet from the ground. She hacked away at the rotten wood so that her whole body shook. Occasionally, she threw herself backwards to release a shower of debris over her shoulder. Without relinquishing her toe-hold on the edge of the hole, she kept working for eight minutes. Then she left for a feed at the feeding place.

A week later, on April 6, she took me by surprise when I found her at least 500 feet from the first hole, excavating a new hole in the top of another rotten poplar stump. She was tremendously busy, yet found time to quiver her wings at Red in a nearby tree and to chase away a chickadee that came along quite innocently. It was as if the hole drilling, first on her agenda, ought to be interrupted by demonstrations which also belonged to the occasion, such as a bit of chasing, so that the ritual might be carried out and in the correct sequence. At any rate, Bluey kept the wheels rolling at a fast clip during the significant pre-nesting activities of this pair. Nest-hole excavating is usually shared by the male red-breasted nuthatch. The assistance Bluey got from her mate may have been sufficient to her, but Red certainly did not give her substantial help in construction.

Four days later I found Bluey back again at the first hole in the old poplar stump. Obviously, her work here had progressed considerably, for she disappeared far into the cavity. Out of sight, she worked in the hole for many long seconds. Then, shuffling along to the entrance, first her upturned bill full of debris appeared, then *she* popped out. With a shake of her head, she cast her load of shavings upon the passing wind.

Red was in attendance, courting her, the feathers of his rump erect, his wings quivering. His crown feathers rose and fell with the rhythm of his excitement, as he sidled to and fro on a branch or up and down the trunk of a tree conveniently near her. And all the while he sang with his bill closed, a whispered song on a high note, *tiiiiiirrrrrr*!

Twelve days later, on April 22, Greenie, a female with a green band on her leg, was excavating a nest chamber in an old poplar stump not far from Bluey's second nesting-hole in the ravine.

By all rules and regulations, Bluey ought by this time to have been laying her first egg in the first hole. Instead she was back again, not lawfully engaged in her own business, but watching Greenie with interest. As Greenie left her hole for a rest, Bluey quivered her wings at her and Greenie responded in kind. With so many onlookers around no wonder that Greenie, a timid soul, hesitated before re-entering her hole. But she finally did and once more set to work deep down inside.

That Bluey's presence at this hole had seemed suspicious to me was fully confirmed when, three days later, I found her in possession of Greenie's hole and nest chamber. As I came along, she popped out and hopped around the opening, plainly proclaiming her ownership. And then popped back in again. From what I now knew of Bluey, I could easily imagine how she had simply waited and slipped in when nobody was looking, and then defied anybody to step over that threshold. Under such circumstances, a braver bird than Greenie would not have had the chance to do anything about it. So Greenie and her mate moved to West Hill, far away from their lost castle. Here in another old poplar stump, they chiselled out a new abode just as fine as the first one.

Knowing that no one may forever transgress with impunity, sooner or later I expected vengeance to fall upon Bluey for her rash popping into houses that did not belong to her. Next I saw her making the mattress, upon which her eggs and young were to nestle snugly, deep down in the usurped nest chamber. The male helped her collect tendrils, dead pine needles and fine birch bark, but he forebore to enter the hole and offered her his share of nesting material at the entrance, where she grasped it and took it inside.

Five days later Red put his seal upon the nest-hole. He came with a glistening ball of pine gum in his bill. This he smeared all around the opening and for a time the gum attached him to the hole with long, elastic, golden threads that were loath to let him go. By his movement and his expression, one was impressed by the importance of this undertaking. It was a task he shared with no one and which required endless inspections and the dabbing on of more gum many times. When finished, the entrance was surrounded by a sticky ring of gum, an inch and a half wide, to which floss and fluff, sailing along on the light spring breezes, fastened and draped themselves, partly covering the hole like ragged gossamer curtains.

Deep inside, behind her mate's seal and sign that read plainly, "Caution! Beware the trap!" Bluey was safe.

There she laid her prescribed clutch of five to seven eggs, speckled with reddish brown and lavender. And eventually, in the fullness of time, she delivered to the world a large and animated family.

Night-Life at Peak Hill

She rose at my feet in a flight so fluttering and erratic that, at first, I could hardly tell whether it was a bird or a piece of brown paper blown by the wind.

It was a whippoorwill. Her size, a little smaller than the blue jay, her winding, noiseless manner of moving, her buff breastband, the shape of her head, half miniature owl, half giant swallow, told me so. She alighted on an old log 10 feet away. With an anxious whimper she ran the length of the log limping, trailing her wing.

She crouched there, never leaving me with her eyes. But I knew her game and refused to be enticed from the spot from which she had risen. It was on the north slope of Peak Hill, a stone's throw from where the hermit thrush sat on a nestful of eggs. Many years ago a bushy spruce had fallen across the slope and now, in mid-summer, 1946, grey lichens covered every naked twig of the old skeleton. Over its mossy resting place a patch of bunchberries in full bloom spread its white-starred pattern and a sweet sugarplum bush gracefully bowed its smooth blue-green leaves towards the flowers and the earth.

I looked around not daring to move. Three feet to my left I saw two white objects. Had they been a trifle smaller they might easily have been mistaken for bunchberry blooms. The whippoorwill whimpered again as she saw my glance turn in their direction. She took off down the slope trailing her wing.

The two white things were the eggs of the whippoorwill. Adorned with a delicate marbled design in umber and tan, they rested without a vestige of other nesting arrangement on a bed of pine needles. It was a miracle my clumsy feet had missed them.

In the hope of seeing the bird return I retired and hid behind a bush. She came after a while, but so softly, so soundlessly, that I found her confronting me unexpectedly. With unblinking eyes fixed in my direction she sat there all of a sudden perched on a bare twig. She said *quoit*. It sounded like a large drop of water falling into a pool.

She sat motionless. She did not crouch *along* the branch as birds of the goatsucker family are wont to do. She perched *across* it and her dwarfed legs did not seem to make the position awkward for her. After well-nigh an hour of immobility she finally wore down my patience and I left to let her return in peace to her eggs.

Peak Hill towers above Pimisi Bay and is the highest hill in the vicinity. Below, the lake looks like blue glass cut out to fit the irregular shoreline. On dewy mornings light mists mark the course of the Mattawa River amongst the blueing hills beyond the lake. On the other side of the Trans-Canada Highway the house nestles under the pines.

It was down there that the whippoorwills had chosen the rock outside our bedroom window as their courtship bower. Every night since the male's first ringing call sounded his return in early May, he came there to proclaim his territorial aspirations. He sat there crouched, his head low, rocking his body gently from side to side, calling loudly over and over again, *chuck-whip-poor-will*, *chuck-whip-poor-will*, *chuck-whip-poor-will*!

But one day the male's calling abruptly changed. At the end of a prolonged sentence the even tempo of his singing was suddenly accelerated to breathless speed.

I crept up to the window. The male was no longer alone. The dim shape of another whippoorwill wheeled down upon the rock and crouched close beside him. It was the female. She lacked the flashing white of the male's breastband and tail feathers. And from then on wherever they were I could tell when the male was no longer alone.

He pressed himself up to her. *Coorah, coorah*, he uttered. He swooped up into the air, displaying, and down on her other side. But she only pressed her breast against the ground. He bowed from side to side and his *coorah* dissolved into cooings, soft, fast, softer, faster.

But the stirrings of her blood did not yet match his. She flew and the male followed in great excitement. On the way he became distracted by a large June bug that buzzed around a tree-top. He dashed in pursuit, hovered an instant like a huge hummingbird on wings beating at invisible speed, caught the insect in his enormous whiskered mouth and disappeared from sight.

A week later I came upon the female sitting alone on the rock. Over the lake a full moon was rising like a giant golden coin. I stood perfectly still, and a moment later the male alighted on another rock at some distance from the female. He cooed softly, flashed the white of his tail feathers. She did not move where she sat not five feet in front of me. Silently the male flew up behind her. She crouched deeper, spread her wings. Lightly, like a butterfly, he descended upon her. Wings rippled, trembled. Then both birds disappeared into the shadows of the trees.

It was apparently the eggs of this pair that I stumbled upon at Peak Hill. An opportunity so rarely granted, I decided to learn more of this bird which sings and mates and lives in the night. For the purpose, I arranged a blind some 10 feet away from the bird, a green-mottled blanket with slits torn in convenient places. Behind it I tucked a folding chair into a young fir tree and covered up my backview with fresh spruce boughs.

That evening, with a flashlight, a watch, and a potent insecticide, I climbed up Peak Hill and slunk as noiselessly as I could into my shelter. The sun, round and flame-red, was just sinking below the horizon. In the twilight, the trees lost their green color and stood like darkened silhouettes against the orange-green sky.

The whippoorwill was sitting motionless on her eggs, like a small mound of dead leaves. She sat just in front of the fallen spruce trunk and a few sprigs of its dead top branches reached out over her. From above, her brown-speckled feather-dress made her invisible and from my blind I had to convince myself she actually was where I knew her to be. She slept with her head tucked under one wing.

All around us the song of the birds had gone into the mighty finale of the day. A hermit thrush was singing from a red pine afire in the last beam of the sun. From time to time ovenbirds rose in exuberant flight songs, brilliantly hued magnolia, myrtle and Nashville warblers flitted from tree to tree, singing, and a bejewelled Canada warbler successfully held his own in the stiff competition. Behind me three Wilson's thrushes challenged the hermit's masterpieces with their golden strains descending the scale.

In my darkened shelter a few black flies hummed against the ceiling, trying to escape the air poisoned by the sprayer. A little deer mouse startled me with the rustle of its feet as it scampered over a rotten log and nervously slipped down a friendly hole further away.

It grew darker. A couple of fireflies flashed their tail-lights across the shadows like tiny comets. The whippoorwill sat on her eggs, deathly still.

Then it happened. From out of the woods behind me an apparition flashed into view. It was the male. He looked like a huge moth, much larger than he really was. His spread tail feathers shone startlingly white. Without a sound he wheeled down towards the female. He alighted in front of her. He pressed his breast to the earth, he edged up to her until bill met bill and he became a perfect looking-glass image of her. He uttered a caressing *coorah*, *coorah* – long-drawn, deliciously tender. He seemed to feed her, but the darkness prevented me from seeing the details of his action. He remained thus in front of her for fully three minutes.

By their eyes, shining red like miniature Chinese lanterns, I could follow the movements of the birds with my flashlight. The illumination did not seem to disturb them. Noiselessly the female flew off the eggs, and it was the first time I saw her leave them of her own volition. The male took her place, turning around tail south. Immovable, he remained on the eggs for a long time.

But presently the male's eyes began to move. He left the eggs which, uncovered, shone white on their pine-needle bed. A second later I heard him calling from Green Woods down below. He tore the silence to shreds. From south, east and west, neighbouring whippoorwills answered him.

The next time I visited Peak Hill it was an hour before dawn. I stumbled through the thick underbrush and climbed the hill guided by my flashlight.

Suddenly, in the pitch darkness, an ovenbird flung himself above the tree-tops in the most magnificent flight song I have ever heard and fell to earth again I knew not where. A couple of whippoorwills called in the distance.

In the beam of the flashlight the humped outline of the whippoorwill showed faintly, her eyes shining red. The woods were sopping wet after a thunderstorm and the mosquitoes were murderous. I sat on my rickety chair writing my notes by feel.

At this early hour the ovenbirds seemed to be moved by some special exultation, for from the woods below, bird after bird rose in thrilling flight song.

A little breeze rustled through the leaves, and died just as a faint light began to show on the horizon. With rare inspiration a hermit thrush began to sing. Then a song sparrow suddenly burst into song. The Wilson's thrushes awakened and a white-throated sparrow surprised the world with the clearest whistle. A little while later a robin gave a *sotto voce* rendering of its theme to begin the day's activity, and from all corners of the land, whippoorwills called vigorously as if they, too, belonged to the daylight parade.

I did not see her go, but as I flashed on my light the whippoorwill was gone. Alone, I sat there and listened to the rising volume of bird song as dawn seeped in through the trees. Every bird was soon awake and singing. There was no movement, only song.

Presently I heard the whippoorwill grunt as she returned from her breakfast flight. She sat blinking on a broken-off birch stump, looking with suspicion at my blanket. Behind us the male called so close that the *chuck* note preceding the *whip-poor-will* was plainly audible. The female fluttered down to the ground and moved sedately up to cover the eggs. Of one accord all the whippoorwills ceased calling.

Another evening at dusk I was back again. The whippoorwill on her eggs and I in my shelter sat motionless for 20 minutes.

Suddenly I heard the bird give a low alarm note, *quoit*. I looked through the slits, wondering why. Without warning, a Cooper's hawk swooped down and alighted on the dry branch that upheld my blind. The branch trembled under its weight. I stared at the hawk with a pang of fear for the bird on her eggs.

It was a magnificent hawk, so close to me that I could see each feather slipping into place as it folded its powerful wings. Slowly the bird turned its head around and our eyes met. The hawk bobbed its head fixing me with its piercing glance; its expression showed plainly as much surprise as I felt at our unexpected face-to-face encounter. The hawk did not like it and took off with such force that my shelter wobbled.

The whippoorwill sat pressed tight on her eggs.

On July 4, 19 days after I discovered the whippoorwills' nesting place, the male flew in upon the sunset scene unusually early. His coming revealed that, at last, the great event had happened for which the birds and I had waited so patiently and eagerly for three weeks. Two small forms moved amongst the feathers of the parents. The male fed the young a generous meal out of his crop while the female watched.

When the mother bird presently disentangled herself from the family group, the male adjusted himself, covering the chicks. He sat motionless for a long time. Then the female returned and fed the youngsters.

By this time I was consumed with desire to take a closer look at the little ones. The moment I stepped out of my shelter the female flushed, grunting and trailing her wing. On the bed of pine needles I beheld the young, two diminutive golden-brown chicks, sitting silent and still in their utter innocence.

On the second day the precocious youngsters moved about freely. One chick stretched himself on his toes and pecked at his mother's bill. She regorged a morsel of food into the yellow-pink cavity opened before her.

But the male was late in coming this evening and the thought of the hawk came uncomfortably to mind. It grew dark and the fireflies began flicking their lights. I left the shelter to reconnoitre.

But as soon as I got out into the open the male flashed into view. He wheeled towards the family, then caught sight of me, made an abrupt turn, and perched on the old tree-stump six feet in front of me.

He said *quoit* twice. He sat staring at me for a long time and I felt as if caught redhanded in a disgraceful act. I tried not to move, but with swarms of angry mosquitoes around my ears it was impossible.

My movement had an electrifying effect. Immediately the male fluffed the feathers on his shoulders menacingly. He let down his wings and trailed them stiff and curved, as he advanced towards me, balancing himself on the branch. He looked like a small owl about to charge.

The tension of the situation grew rapidly and suddenly another involuntary movement on my part touched off the spark. Everything happened at once. The female wheeled backwards off the young, whining, trailing her wing, and the male took to the air with a great flutter. *Quoit, quoit* came sharply and threateningly from in front, from behind me. The male moved like lightning. He hovered here, there, just above my head, on vibrating wings. The chicks pressed themselves to the ground, motionless.

By this time I felt there had been enough excitement and I beat an inglorious retreat down the hill in the darkness. The male followed. I had flashlight glimpses of his eyes shining red and as I finally reached the house he was outside the window calling emphatically.

When the youngsters were three days old I found the original nesting site empty, but the female flushed startlingly close to my feet. This time the chicks dispersed while the female ran off, grunting and trailing her wing.

One young sat pressed against the trunk of the fallen spruce. As I picked it up it rolled over in my hand as if dead. Still covered with golden-brown down, the bird's pin-feathers were beginning to show and the eyes were opening.

Half an hour later the female returned. She crouched in a hollow not far from the pine needle bed. She called softly, *kjok, kjok*, a new note I had not heard. When she got no response she took wing and visited first the little one under the fallen spruce and then the other hidden under the bunchberries. Then she went back and crouched in the hollow. From there she called again, *kjok* ... The next moment a rippling motion zigzagged through the bunchberries from the fallen spruce to the parent bird in the hollow, and downy youngster number one nestled under the wing of its mother. Another ripple, and chick number two scurried unseen to the haven.

When the male appeared he was apparently unaware of his family having moved out. He flew down to the old nesting site. He searched and searched, flopping about in the bunchberries. The female saw him and rose from the hollow, where-upon the father happily rejoined his lost family. From then on the birds moved into a new place every night. By the fifth day the chicks were beginning to lose their golden-brown natal down and it was being replaced by the lovely whippoorwill patterns of wood-browns, buff and black.

When the youngsters were 13 days old, I found them more than 100 feet from their birthplace. They were now hopping about in long leaps like frogs, and I had no difficulty catching them. From the tips of their tails to the tips of their bills they measured a little over four and a half inches. They would need another four or five inches before they were fully grown, most of which they would acquire by the full development of their tail feathers.

It was on this day that the youngsters showed fear for the first time. A special warning note from the mother, as she sat not far away watching me and the chick in my hand, seemed to release the reaction. As if obeying a command, the young one began struggling violently, answering his mother in a loud babyish voice. Finally, he wrenched himself free, fluttered a couple of yards on unpractised wings, and disappeared under a leaf of bracken.

The next day I returned once more to Peak Hill but searched in vain for the whippoorwill family. Now the young ones could fly and the birds were gone. The nesting season was at an end.

A whippoorwill called loudly, insistently. Drifting down the river in the canoe an evening in the 1940s, I sat spellbound. Through the translucence of the twilight hour, the jagged, sharply etched black silhouettes of the cliffs and the forest trees along the shores were slowly passing in review. Aft, the V-shaped ripples in the wake of the light craft marvellously reflected the fading light.

Goatsuckers — birds of the night and the twilight hours! Secretive? Are they? They belong to the crepuscule part of the 24 hours. Perhaps it was natural that they should arouse the curiosity of the early settlers! Superstitious they were, and this was an exciting mystery! What did these birds do so late at night? Their loud calls, their frequent visits to the pastures, the regularity of their habits? These birds were voracious insect-eaters, and there were myriads of insects around the cattle. "The goat was dry this morning, when I came to milk her." Was it? "Yes, and three mornings ago too! And that enormous whiskered mouth . . . with hardly any beak to speak of! Goatsuckers!" What better name could have been invented for birds of such mysterious habits?

The sound of the whippoorwill's call skittered across the water as my canoe slid noiselessly, borne on the breast of the lazy current out into wide-open expanse of the night-shadowed lake. Another one called – then a third, and a fourth one. Considerable distances separated one from the other. Their lands were of spacious dimensions. Beautifully graded from *fortissimo* to the faintest *pianissimo* their voices came through the evening air. In this large untouched land there were many whippoorwills in those days. The forests were young. Carpets of dry leaves and fir needles covered the ground, sheltering undergrowth grew in the open woodlands. In a forest like this one, which had been left in its natural state and which had not yet had time to grow tall and dark toward its inevitable climax, large moths, such as June bugs and cecropias, came alive in the late spring and early summer. Conditions there were perfect for the whippoorwills and their chicks, due to hatch three weeks from the day the two eggs were laid in the early week of June.

Goatsuckers! Still another species of the same family inhabited this forest. Both were birds of the twilight, highly insectivorous of habit, but mutually separated by occupying entirely different habitats. High in the still light-flooded evening sky, the night-hawks course hither and yon. Skilled aerial performers, their slender pointed wings whip the air in unevenly rhythmic beats. Their whiskered mouths wide agape, they hawk the night-flying insects, and from their exultant heights their cries come faintly, at short even intervals. Tremulous booms reverberate through the air as one of the birds drops dizzily like a stone to a lower level, to recover smartly the next instant and resume its interrupted flight.

In the days of the past such a number of night-hawks were there to be seen in the evening sky over the lake of Pimisi Bay

– often a dozen or more, some coming from distances, but most being residents of the area.

In this natural environment, atop one of the tallest cliffs, I came upon a breeding pair. On a flat rock covered with grey lichens lay their two eggs. And when in due time they hatched, the two beautifully patterned light grey and dark-striped chicks could only be discerned with difficulty as they moved about in their lichen-grown surroundings. The chicks, like those of the whippoorwills, precociously developed at hatching time, are for a while guarded and supported by their parents, until one day, dressed in their new plumages of wood-browns, black and white, like that of their parents, they are able to shift for themselves.

Strange that this interesting family of birds should, as they did, practically vanish from this area! Only a remnant of the once-so-common whippoorwills now remains scattered thinly through the woodlands. The process was gradual, at first hardly noticeable, until one day we suddenly woke up to the fact. After that, if in one year we did not hear any whippoorwills calling, it did not necessarily mean that they were gone for good. Fluctuations in animal populations always occur from time to time for various reasons, not always connected with any serious decline in numbers. This is usually followed by recoveries, sometimes spectacular. Each spring-time at dusk we listened intently lest, by chance, any distant calls be missed.

The calling of the whippoorwills is most frequent and emphatic during the beginning of the nesting season. Competition is a recognized prompter of pronounced bird behaviour. But now, for several years, there has been none. And while, during the past decade and a half, whippoorwills have irregularly occupied the dry newly cut-over area a mile or so south of Pimisi Bay, the nearly unbroken silence in recent years in this benign whippoorwill habitat has been depressing.

The night-hawks' decline at first seems to have been more sudden, with a slight recovery later on. Odd individuals, or, more rarely, a small party of them, have over the years been spotted in the evening sky over the lake. But where they came from is guesswork. The cliff-nesting night-hawks left long since. Several years ago a pair of ravens started raising their broods from a large stick nest they built on a cliff ledge above the river, making the neighbourhood uncomfortable for the lesser breeds. During the last two decades, on an auspicious evening in early September, I might have happened upon two or three of those sudden migratory streams, previously so common, of night-hawks chasing insects at high speed over a river, lake or field, darting erratically to and fro as they went, only to disappear a few minutes later as if they had never been there.

Speculation on the reasons underlying the decline of the goatsuckers is idle. The possibilities are many and their interactions difficult to trace and to define. Among them are changes in the environment, due simply to the natural growth of woodlands and forest, which thus overreach the norms of these birds' habitat requirements; the undue encroachment upon their living room by other species; natural declines, shifts and changes, or catastrophes affecting the numerical stability of the insectlife upon which these birds depend; the far-reaching effects of chemicals; or civilization's obstructions increasingly erected in the way of the migrating birds, causing often appalling mortality. Extensive scientific research is needed to weigh these different circumstances and determine their interrelated potentialities.

Beyond this looms the problems of conservation. How to define the essence of this balanced relationship between living things and their environment, upon which all development, indeed all life, hinges? In the strong competition with so highly developed a species as mankind, where do you start conserving? How do you maintain it? How do you reconcile the highly conflicting interests of the environment, wildlife (animal and plantlife), and the prolific technology-ridden human being?

The Apartments

What first attracted the pileated woodpeckers to the quaking aspen is not easy to say. Perhaps it was the tree's splendid 60-foot height and its diameter measured at breast height of no less than 14 inches. Or the small round hole on the trunk's north-east side, where a pair of yellow-bellied sapsuckers had nested a few years before. Or the dry sticks that stood out naked against the sky above the aspen's still voluminous crown foliage. An aspen grows only so tall in so many years before reaching its prime. And then begins the decline – dry sticks at the top, rot starting at the core, and the wood becoming soft enough deep inside for a woodpecker to carve out its gourdlike cavity.

The male pileated woodpecker alighted 42 feet up on the tree's exposed south side. He clung there for a while, then his measured peckings resounded loudly through the forest. His resplendent scarlet crest shook lightly with the effort of each mighty strike. And the sun played upon the great bird's shiny black feather-dress with faint multi-coloured reflections.

Presently the woodpecker stopped pecking and gave a loud call, *cuk* . . . *cuk* . . . *cuk*. It sounded almost like a burst of big loud laughter. Far away from the west came an answering call. The male listened. He waited, sat, and waited. But before the caller was even in sight, off he dashed on mighty wing-beats, crest flat over the crown of his head, the neck with its white stripe stretched full-length.

The two birds met on a tall stub of another aspen long dead. The male drummed, at first slow big pecks, then faster like a drill, intense, sharp taps. The sound excited the female and she dashed off. Both vanished.

This engaging reciprocal play of drumming and dashing around, back and forth to the nest-hole to peck there a bit, went on for several days. The birds' silver-lined black wings beat the air with a swishing sound; their claws, as they alighted *plunk* on a tree-trunk, scraped and scratched upon the rough bark; and call answered call, loudly, emphatically.

But as the hole in the aspen became larger and a little deeper, gradually the birds' interest in it increased and, in like measure, their vehemence and excitement about each other abated. By the time the male slipped inside the hole for the first time and turned around, the two birds had reached a stage where they came and went, worked and relieved each other at the nest in a well-balanced rhythmic routine. Soon they had the cavity gouged out into its final shape, ready to receive the clutch of white eggs.

On a day in the beginning of May when the new light green leaves of the aspen rustled for the first time in the soft spring breeze, the woodpecker pair settled down to their regular sessions of warming the eggs. All night the male slept on them and soon after the break of dawn the female flew in to relieve him for her longest session of the day, as if to make up for the time lost during the night. After that there was no haste or hurry in their alternate comings and goings, no noise, except the air swishing through their feathers as they flew in and out at the shifts.

And only on these occasions did excitement grip them briefly. The mate's loud call from a distance alerted the bird inside. By the time grasping claws scratched the bark of the trunk, it was on its feet with the shadow of its head playing faintly on the wall of the corridor between cavity and doorway. Quickly, once or twice, the arriving bird's head swept across the oval opening like the shutter of a camera. This was the signal. Out shot the bird inside, past its side-stepping mate. And by the time it was flapping its way to distant feeding grounds, the relieving bird had already popped inside and was covering the eggs as if no break had occurred.

In this benign season nothing untoward happened to prevent the success of the pileated woodpeckers' nesting. By the end of June the whole family was out and coursing the forest. Lest they miss the provisioned meal, the fledglings gave loud calls that echoed amongst the trees to inform the parents of their whereabouts. With soft notes and its gullet full of food, a parent approached to fill the gaping mouth of each impatient beggar about once every hour. In another week the whole family was off and away in search of other feeding grounds. And the quaking aspen stood alone with the large oval hole gaping on the south side of its trunk.

Months later, in the late fall of 1969, the male pileated woodpecker returned, and on the aspen's west side about 10 feet below the level of the south hole excavated a snug winter dormitory for himself. The waning light provided the cue for his goodnight ritual. From distant feeding areas he came flying soon after sundown – about 10 to 20 minutes earlier on dull and very cold days – and slipped inside so quickly and unobtrusively that he was seldom seen.

Then in March, without any reference to his mate, the male pileated woodpecker decided on the site for the new nest-hole. He tapped the first chisel mark of the doorway-to-be at a place about nine feet above and slightly more west of the first hole in the south side. And surprisingly, for it is not often so among woodpeckers, his initial decision proved to be irrevocable.

So far so good. But when the male attempted to transmit the important message to the female, her unwillingness – whatever was her motivation – to accept his decision almost wrecked his scheme. He resorted to every means of persuasion. He drummed at the site, spaced taps, alternating with strumming, short, fast taps. When in response to this signal the female arrived, he went into an elaborate tapping ritual at the edge of the would-be doorway, *tap . . . tap . . . tap*, his bill tapping stiffly under his breast, his scarlet crest erect, trembling, and his wings opened ever so slightly. The female promptly copied every move to the last detail.

But no, this was not the place *she* fancied for the nest! And off she flew, leaving him to tap and to strum and to bore his hole alone. For days he chased after the female. For days he drummed and he strummed. But still she would not listen.

Meanwhile, the male had the hollow well started. Presently he was able to disappear inside to the tip of his spiked tail. And only then did the female begin to show signs of interest. She came, she looked, she watched, she answered his calls. And once she reached this stage, it did not take her long to finally accept the situation, to go in, and to start working upon the cavity herself.

The pileated woodpeckers were incubating their full clutch of eggs when a pair of sapsuckers, after a great deal of fuss and ceremony, decided to nest in a hole which the male had already started in the adjacent aspen. The dry, giveaway top branches of this tree also advised of advanced core rot and, shortly after, a belated spring wind broke off the top and left it dangling down the side of the trunk. Soon, with red crest on end and red throat patch fluffed, the male sapsucker could be seen scattering billfuls of brownish chips upon the air with quick shakes of the head. A week or so later his female deposited her eggs, one a day, on a small collection of fragrant sawdust left on the bottom of the cavity.

About the same time, in the woods across the clearing by a small noisy creek, a pair of yellow-shafted flickers laid their eggs in a hole they had nested in the year before, near the top of a rotting birch stub. Five days they had been sitting on the eggs when a red squirrel discovered the doorway and smelled the eggs. Eagerly the squirrel tore at the rotten wood just at the place where the eggs lay inside the wall on the bottom of the cavity. But the wood held. Frustrated, he ran up to the doorway – where a mighty jab from the flicker's beak sent him sprawling to the ground.

For two days the flickers fought a brave fight for nest and eggs, but it was a losing battle. The red squirrel, never

inclined to give up easily, by sheer chance hit upon the rare moment when both flickers were absent. He slipped in, naturally, and ate all the eggs but one that crashed to the ground.

In their search for a new place to nest the flickers came to the quaking aspen. They saw the doorway of the pileated woodpecker's winter dormitory. They inspected the cavity, found it suitable and in need of little fixing. To them this was important, because the season was already far advanced.

The sapsuckers at first met the intrusion of the flickers with hostility. By this time their young had hatched. This created a sensitive situation, for as the parents began bringing food and their movements gave the site of the nest away, the risk of its being detected by predators increased. And with that, naturally, the birds' nervous tension and their intolerance of intruders also increased.

But the flickers were in a hurry and sought no quarrels. With the laying of the first egg they became secretive and avoided all brash behaviour. Moreover, the sapsuckers operated on a lower level than the flickers. And with their respective doorways facing in opposite directions, occasions for clashes became practically non-existent.

The maintenance of peace between the pileated woodpeckers on the third floor and the flickers never became a problem because of the slow rhythm observed by both pairs, and a well-timed shuttle service at both nests that effectively kept the tenants out of each others' feathers. Nor did the loud chatter of the pileated youngsters at the top, transmitted to the flickers by tree-trunk radio, disturb them. Only occasionally, when the adult pileated woodpeckers were absent, might a flicker be seen hopping up to the large oval doorway to look in.

By June 30 the two young ones in the pileated woodpeckers' nest were ready for their pre-emergence rites. The black and white stripes running along their undulating necks and their slim heads with their light grey bills wide open, calling or begging or just panting, gave them a distinctly reptilian look. Each time a parent arrived to feed them and then departed, their excitement knew no bounds. Eagerly, roughly, they pushed each other from the coveted advance position at the edge of the doorway, often just missing a fall into space. But in spite of all near-misses the final tumbling-out did not take place until the cool of the next morning.

A few days afterward, the sapsuckers' nestlings fledged. With that the flickers had the premises to themselves. And three weeks later, in the early morning of July 27, they finally brought their second nesting attempt to a successful conclusion.

The following winter the male pileated woodpecker again took up nightly residence in the quaking aspen, this time in nest-hole number one which he had excavated two years ago, while the female took over his west-side sleeping hole where the flickers had nested.

In the spring, as early as March 12, the male was already busy excavating a new hole facing south-east, 25 feet from the ground, his fourth in the quaking aspen. The weather was sunny and soft and the snow, never very deep that winter, was fast disappearing, giving promise of an early spring.

Two weeks later a pair of starlings arrived and began casting covetous eyes on the holes in the aspen.

Starlings have an artful way of expropriating the cavities drilled by the native hole-dwellers, characterized by a kind of pseudo-timid but tenacious obstructiveness. They arrive and they sit and they watch. No aggressive behaviour, no contentiousness. These manoeuvres first arouse in the rightful owners an uneasiness that gradually changes to irritation, then to fear mingled with anger, and these reactions increase in intensity as the season advances. But the starlings are not in any hurry. With admirable patience they wait for their chance. Gradually they become more daring. They inspect the cavity when nobody is looking, enter it and begin throwing out whatever is in it. The bird in the hole is almost invincible.

The pileated woodpeckers stood the strain of the passive menace for awhile. But when two other starlings turned up to join the first pair, they abandoned the fourth hole and began excavating another in a tree 30 feet north of the aspen. To this tree the starlings also came to sit and look and wait. Enough of this! The woodpeckers quit and flew away to an old stub where they hurriedly began enlarging a hole once inhabited by a pair of hairy woodpeckers.

Had the fierce windstorm a week or so later not toppled this old stub, the pileated woodpeckers probably would never have returned to the aspen grove. But when once again, homeless, they arrived at the place, it seemed to be abandoned. The starling visitors had left, and the first pair – *hush, hush* – were sitting on newlaid eggs in the west hole, the flickers' ex-nest. The pileated woodpeckers' unfinished hole in the aspen's sister tree gaped at them invitingly. Not there, but seven feet above it, they began boring another hole. In this one the female eventually laid her eggs, and in due time the pair successfully fledged from it a family of three.

Meanwhile, the flickers returned from migration and so did the sapsuckers. The latter had little difficulty settling upon a nest site. Everything was there to attract them, familiar surroundings, their old hole from last year, and they bored their new hole just two feet above it.

But the flickers, having two previous home localities to choose from, one in the aspen and the other in the woods across the clearing, spent some time hesitating, flying from one place to the other – long enough, in fact, for the starlings to usurp their ex-hole in the aspen. That forced the decision upon the flickers and they nested in a tree across the clearing. But as in the previous year, this nesting also ended in disaster.

Now where would the flickers go? How strong is the attraction of the tree once used! How enticing is the familiar locality and the gaping hole beckoning!

All was quiet at the aspen when the flickers, hesitating several times, finally looked into the west hole. Except for some soiled nesting materials it was empty. The starlings were gone. But as if their occupation had attached to the hole some kind of miasma, the flickers would not go into it. Gingerly one of them hopped up to the pileated woodpeckers' empty hole at the top and looked in. But the flicker did not enter that one either. Then they discovered the hole the pileated woodpeckers had started on the south-east side of the trunk early in March. Forthwith they set about finishing it and there they laid their eggs.

About a week before the flickers had come to nest in the aspen again, a slender brown duck came flying surreptitiously and quickly from across the lake on rapid wings, neck outstretched and a little tuft of a reddish crest showing at the back of her head. It was a hooded merganser. For some reason of her own she abruptly altered course and sped in a circle out over the lake again, and then flew straight to the aspen. She rounded the stout broken-off branch by the pileated wood-peckers' first nest-hole – and the hole literally swallowed her.

For four long weeks the little brown duck performed her rapid sorties and fly-ins directly and unhesitatingly to mark her infrequent recesses from incubating her collection of eggs at the bottom of the cavity. She appeared and she vanished like an arrow, and the hole 42 feet up on the aspen's south side gaped seemingly empty. Who would see her? Who would know she was there? Not the flickers low down on the east side of the tree, absorbed as they were in their slow-rhythm attendance upon their eggs, and then upon their young ones.

On July 7 a wisp of dark downy feathers fluttered in the doorway of the duck's secret residence. And that was all, all that remained to tell of the ducklings' dramatic descent on spread but unpinioned wings and extended webbed feet into the thistles below. And two weeks later the flickers brought out another late brood from their second successful nesting in the grand old aspen.

Thus, aptly, by the simple means of cycles, rhythm, and timing, nature fits its jigsaw patterns of individual lives together into an interlocking harmonious whole. And the one life appropriately and unwittingly serves the other.

The venerable quaking aspen had not yet seen the last of its usefulness. It was important, of course, that its apartments attract a select clientele that could take care of themselves in so risk-filled a locality as this inviting forest edge interposed between the natural wilderness and the unnatural highway, with its increasingly dense traffic of insensitive mechanical devices coursing heedlessly east and west. And there were no accidents.

The year after the above-related events took place, the hooded merganser with her elegant nape fringe and her secretive darting ways returned to lay her eggs in the same hole in the old aspen, uttering her breathy *prrt, prrt*. Exactly what she meant I would not guess, but when she happened to espy me watching her quick flights in and out of the nest-hole, she repeated the soft notes.

That same year, when the duck and the flicker pair were the two other tenants of the aspen, a female American kestrel, formerly called sparrow hawk, became interested in the pileated woodpeckers' dormitory. The handsome falcon pair, he in shades of russet, blue-grey and beige, white and black, spotted and striped, she larger, browner, investigated the locality thoroughly while engaged in some preliminary courtship. Quickly they decided it would do all right, and forthwith the female began refurbishing the former dormitory according to her own specifications. I don't know if at this time the falcons were aware of their co-tenants. But, as the flickers' entrance opened east and the duck's south, high above the tree's middle, while the falcons' entrance faced west, there were few opportunities for any hostile encounters.

For the kestrels, the smallest of our American falcons, which lacked the tools to do their own excavation, the cavity of the dormitory had with multiple uses become comfortably roomy. And that year and the next the pair successfully raised two broods of young in it. Fast, watchful and alert, highly positive in behaviour, the falcons gave something of fresh purpose and efficiency to the environment. The rights-of-way along the highway became their favourite hunting ground, where they kept the mice population strictly in check. They also caught insects, the large moths, and, occasionally, a small unwary bird. When the young ones finally reached the age of emergence, they could be seen standing in the entrance side by side, two engaging round-eyed gnomes waiting for a meal, waiting for the time to come for the daring leap into fledglinghood.

Two weeks after the falcons' last brood left the nest, a violent tornado-like storm swept through the area on a narrow path. The old aspen stood right in the middle of it. The wind wrung the tree's top-half section off and with its end still attached to the break, the piece crashed down. Around it was havoc.

The old aspen's hospitality probably is a record. During the last four years of its 70-odd years of life, it had played host to six species of birds. Three of these, all belonging to the woodpecker family, bored the five apartments. And from them five pairs and one mother launched no less than nine successful families out of 10 nestings.

Part Three

Second Insight:
Listen...

There should need to be no introduction. Even the most insensate, lacking the ear for consonance, or the knowledge of or the least interest in birds, but finding himself exposed to the song of a wood thrush, could not escape a sympathetic reaction to its pure music. Other circumstances too – the mystery of the singer, the enchantment of the surroundings, the mood of the season – might well augment the sweetness of the moment. And he would walk away with an imprint upon his mind of a fresh natural spontaneity, of a truth simple and direct, not too easily erased. For it is not only the bird's phrasing, the composition and the delivery, that are un-equalled. There is the setting no artist can reproduce, except as a work of highly oversimplified quality. There are the trees, the colourings, the background sounds, the accompaniment, the luminosity of the sky and the clouds reflected delicately –

in other words, a total combination of the beautiful in which everything blends, everything belongs, the lovely and the wild with a purpose and a meaning.

So the portals open wider. From the overwhelming wealth of new impressions awareness grows, and with this the ability to separate and to distinguish. The twittering and the call note, what meaning do they carry, what purpose beyond the individual's momentary mood or its urge that impelled the uttering? I note that it is linked to the bird's movement, to a distinct situation, and realize that there is a coherence.

I am speaking of the woodland song-birds. Hatching in the north, they travel south in winter and return in spring. The males are in the vanguard of the migratory flocks. When they arrive on the breeding grounds, they announce their presence by song. Song is their means of self-expression. From various perches which they visit repeatedly, they sing their special territorial song and thus demarcate the living room they need for reproduction. With bill lifted to the heavens, opening and shutting, the notes pour from the bird's throat loudly and emphatically. And this song carries a twofold message – the first, directed at trespassers of the bird's own species, a warning of occupancy and the risks of intrusion, and the second, directed at the passing female of a male in residence here. This perching song is usually brief, repeated again and again. In spite of its composition often being rich in variations, it is distinct for the species and a means of positive identification. The song rarely develops into a remarkable avian soliloquy, as the rose-breasted grosbeak is inclined to allow it to do, dreamy in tempo, the bird perched high in the spiked top of a balsam fir, the sound of its softly modulated notes dissipated freely into the four winds, going on and on with only the briefest intervals between the strophes.

Later, even as it becomes more select and less frequent, the male's singing acquires subtle nuances. As a rule, the closer the partners of a pair find themselves the less the male sings. There comes a time when the division of their duties at the nest separate them. The male, preoccupied with territorial concerns, patrols the premises, while the female is busy building the nest, laying the eggs and incubating them. And then the male's song forms a bond of communication between them.

During this phase of the nesting cycle some of the most impressive bird song is often to be heard. As already mentioned, the rose-breasted grosbeak is one of the master singers. The sexes share the duties at the nest. The male helps with the building of it; he also incubates the eggs in relays. The female also sings, but her performance is not comparable to the male's. Once I came upon this flamboyantly plumaged male bird sitting on the nest, his crimson chest with its white and black plumage contrasting startlingly with the fresh sun-dappled green foliage of early June. The bird was singing softly. The song stopped, he had seen me. After I quickly withdrew, he sang again. It was the most perfect *sotto voce* rendering of the rose-breasted grosbeak's theme I have ever heard. Like dewdrops, the mellow notes fell. And then, as the female appeared to relieve her mate, in a crescendo his voice rose to full force. He flew from the nest into a tall tree near by and thence filled the air with a prolonged deliciously mellifluous evening song.

Given by the bird entirely on the wing, the flight song is another variation. It is performed over a period including the courtship, the egg-laying and the incubation. Some flight songs are prolonged twittering and warbling compositions given while the bird circles on shallow fluttering wing-beats over a certain significant area, usually where the female is. Another may be described as an exotic varied tonal outpouring performed while the bird – such as the skylark – as if driven by an unnamed force rises into the sky singing and singing without end. Yet another flight song is like the ovenbird's: the bird, singing dramatically, rises high into the air, the next instant to drop stone-like, unresisting, still singing, back to earth. Performed irregularly at any time of day or night, the flight song of the ovenbird, for example, lasts two seconds at the most to become instantly erased as if it never happened. Why? But the seeming passion of it . . . ?

After the eggs hatch, when the attention of the parents is centred on the nest and the feeding of the young requires all their efforts, song is usually suspended altogether.

Enchanted Singer
of the Tree-Tops

One of my favourites among birds is the red-eyed vireo. I know him well and he appeals to me particularly because in looks and comportment he is such a smooth and elegant bird. Slow motion is his specialty, but sometimes he is brimming with nervous energy and moves faster than the arrow in a streamlined fashion all his own. I do not think that the epithet "sluggish," so often used about him, fits him particularly well. It seems to me that we shall need to find another and a better word, one that contains the elements of sobriety and fluidity.

About his singing, terms have been used that are not altogether complimentary – monotonous, repetitious, preacher-like – and I was always inclined to question the aptness of these descriptions. Was he as tireless as his reputation would have him? When in the day did he start singing, when did he stop? Was there any relation between his manner of singing and his character which, if known, would dispel the impression of what might seem monotonous and repetitious? Were his moods, needs, and temperament reflected in the nuances of tone, in the speed and the manner of the delivery of his songs? What I hitherto knew of the red-eyed vireo's singing gave only part of the answer to these questions.

When the call came from the British ornithologist, Noble Rollin, to make an all-day study of some special bird activity, I thought this was a fine opportunity to devote to the red-eye. Everything fitted in very well, too, because the day I was able to do the survey was May 27, 1952, a few days after Male "A" had taken up territory in my study area. At this time my bird was still without a mate and there would, presumably, be few claims upon his attention other than singing and feeding.

Pre-dawn, the most enchanting and mysterious moment in the 24 hours, reigned when I came out at 3:00 a.m. A soft, misty light prevailed, the delicate luminosity of the night, not enough to see but enough to surmise the outlines of the trees and the opening in the woods through which the trail led. A whippoorwill called at close quarters, a loud song, passionate of tempo, for he was in the midst of his love-making. I counted 37 *whip-poor-will*s; then silence. Then he began again.

I walked into the vireo territory, armed with notebook and flashlight and wearing a warm sweater. It was chilly, the temperature was only 43° F, and the wind light from the west. A faint streak of dawn appeared at the eastern horizon, stealing the light from the stars.

Across my path, two veeries began calling, soft interrogative notes that never waited for an answer. Then, muted like a heavenly whisper, the thrushes began to sing. Penetrating the dusk and hanging deliciously upon the air, these whisperings seemed unearthly, but they represented the most potent reality of these birds' lives. For this was the time when competition between the males was strong, when pairing took place and nesting locations were chosen, when the blood within them ran fast and their sensations were acute.

A purple finch flew over, *tuck*ed, and gave a burst of song sweeter than honey. His season was a little ahead of the veeries', beyond the culmination of passions, and his song, therefore, was like an afterthought, a reminiscence of what had stirred in him before the nest-building and the laying of the first eggs.

As the light increased, the singing of the veeries became louder and intermingled with the weirdest discordant notes and exclamations, suggesting an excitement which intensified with the approach of the day. Startling and strange was this conversation between the thrushes, as it emanated explosively from the depths of the underbrush close to the path where I stood, now here, now over there. Then, all of a sudden, the swish of rapid flight low through the bushes from one place to another. Since their beginning, these rituals and displays, these unanswered and unanswerable queries from one tawny thrush to the other, evolved into the charming game I just now witnessed.

But no vireo was yet awake.

Beyond the valley of the spring, the rose-breasted grosbeak began to sing, songs so deliciously lyrical that the bird itself seemed loath to end such a fine performance and took to its wings, the better to enact an accomplished finale. In the top of a green birch, the robin caught the theme of the grosbeak's utterance, but geared it down to a song modulated to reach the ear of a mate sitting quietly on well-incubated eggs. For at this moment, the robin's song was not one of territorial announcement or self-assertion but symbolized the bond between two closely attached creatures.

Light came and at 4:00 a.m. I could see to write without the flashlight. During the next 22 minutes, the number of birds that had testified their awakening rose to 20. A pair of yellow-bellied sapsuckers breakfasted on the sap of a white birch before resuming work on their nest-hole. A crow flew over, welcomed by no one, but busy on its own nest and eggs. A porcupine, climbing an aspen for a feed of green bark, sounded to me like a black bear, and a great blue heron flew over my head and croaked so loudly that, weak-kneed, I nearly sat down on the spot.

By this time, had I not known that my vireo was somewhere on this piece of land whereupon I stood, I would have despaired of his intention ever to sing again. But then, surprisingly (because I had waited so long), exactly nine minutes before sunrise, the red-eyed vireo serenely began dropping phrase upon phrase of song into the confusion of all the other bird voices. With such casual dreaminess did this

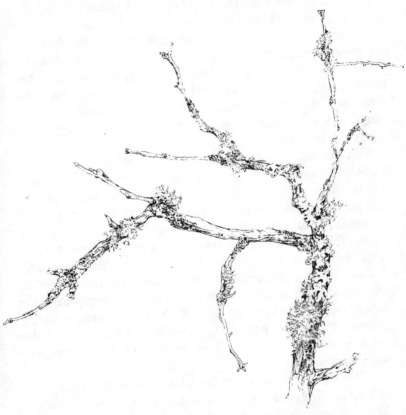

long-awaited awakening happen that it required some seconds to penetrate into my consciousness, and forced me to start counting his inaugural sets of two or three notes at 4:22 a.m.

I found him high in the crown of a trembling aspen. There he wandered about, hopping from twig to twig, looking around, up and down, from side to side. His bill opened and shut, his throat bubbled, and his crest rose lightly and fell with the rhythm of his melody. He sang, phrase following upon phrase, with just enough interval to mark a disconnection between them. He sang with an aloof intensity and confluence that seemed to divorce his performance totally from any special objectives and reasons. This bird sang simply because self-expression in song was as much a part of his being as his red eye.

In the next 100 minutes, when the birds filled the woods with the greatest volume of music, our vireo achieved all his vocal records of the day. Thus, from 5:00 to 6:00 a.m., he sang the greatest number of songs in any hour – 2,155 phrases. From 4:22 a.m., just as he began singing, to 5:00 a.m., he attained his highest speed of delivery, an average of nearly 44 songs per minute; from 6:05 to 6:10 a.m., he sang the most songs in any five-minute period of the day, an average of 70 songs per minute.

Yet, breathless would not properly describe the performance of this bird. He continued to sing for the next three hours with a perfectly calm and casual continuance that at the end amassed him a total of 6,063 songs, delivered at a speed of 40 songs per minute. During this time, he allowed himself six pauses from one to six minutes each, which he divided equally among the three hours. While he sang, he wandered leisurely from one part of his territory, an area less than three acres, to the other, selecting his way through the foliated crowns of the tallest aspens and birches. Had his trail not been so clearly marked by song, it would have been a problem to follow this bird, which moved at such heights and blended so well with his surroundings.

Although my vireo often fed while he sang, and sang with his mouth full, more concentrated feeding called for silence, and the important business of preening claimed all his attention. Once a trespassing vireo, a stranger, interrupted him. Abruptly he stopped singing and, like an arrow released from a taut bow, he shot down from his tall perch directly in pursuit of the intruder. With that the incident closed. With his only red-eyed neighbour settled on an adjacent territory to the north, my vireo had no altercations. On one occasion during the afternoon, the two happened to come close to their common border at the same time; but from this nothing more serious resulted than that the birds for about a quarter of an hour indulged in competitive singing.

A little before 9:00 in the morning, the vireo stopped singing. Up to this time he had spent almost four out of four and a half hours singing continuously.

This was a remarkable record as, apart from the need of advertising himself and his territory, nothing had occurred to call forth extraordinary vocal efforts on his part. Red-eyed vireos do not always sing as persistently as this bird did, especially during the first days after arrival from the south, when leisurely feeding is often the keynote of existence to many of them. Nor do all individuals possess the same capacity for vocal expression. I have known at least one other red-eyed vireo whose total number of songs in a day, even at the most exciting period, probably never reached four figures. (As to the pursuit of the strange vireo, I surmised that this was a passing female, because the male *stopped singing* and dashed off, chasing it, instead of challenging it by voice and gesture. That nothing came of it only suggests that, for the female, the moment was not auspicious.)

The next half-hour my bird spent feeding and preening. He descended from the heights of the tree crowns to the middle strata of the woods, where, one may presume, he found more privacy in the secluded leafy niches. Then, once again, he resumed singing. While he still attained a speed of 38 songs when he sang, his average from 9:00 to 10:00 a.m. was only six songs a minute for the whole hour. This proved to be an interesting fact, because regardless of his hourly averages, his speed of singing consistently and gradually declined through-out the day — in other words, he sang more and more slowly as the day advanced.

After his hour of rest, the vireo achieved a forenoon peak of singing that lacked only 13 songs in reaching as high a total as that obtained from 5:00 to 6:00 a.m. He worked up to this peak in the hour before noon, but would, I think have reached it earlier had he not wandered into a grove of trees heavily infested with the forest tent caterpillar. Here he distracted himself with a great deal of flycatching on the wing. If his objective was the eating of the tachinia flies, which prey upon the tent caterpillars, this activity from a human viewpoint may not have been useful. But, of course, I could not be sure these actually were the insects he caught. As to the caterpillars, my vireo tramped lightly over the mass of them. Few birds relish these hairy worms. But, as I watched the shadow of a wriggling caterpillar on a translucent leaf, the vireo snapped it up, dashed it to pulp on a twig at his feet and ate it.

From dawn till noon, the vireo had reached a grand total of 14,027 songs, but after this his singing diminished notably. The interruptions between groups of songs became longer and more frequent, even as he sang more and more slowly. From noon until going to roost, he gave only a little more than half as many songs as during the early part of the day. But even this was a remarkable number. And his voice continued to be heard when most of the other birds sang but little, or were altogether silent. Moreover, compared with the all-day record of 6,140 songs of an unmated European blackbird, made by Noble Rollin on April 5, 1948, my vireo's performance during the afternoon alone exceeded this total by 2,030 songs.

The lower peak of singing, which occurred during the afternoon, may have been due to the encounter at the territorial border with the neighbouring red-eye to the north. For quite a while, certainly, this stimulated both birds to greater vocal effort. But the time of afternoon rest came in the next two hours, when my vireo wandered about within a small area, or fed, or sat on a twig trimming and polishing every feather in his plumage, and sang only a little.

The last hour of his day the vireo spent in the top of a quaking aspen. Here he moved from perch to perch. I saw the easy opening and closing of his bill and heard his notes drop, one by one, upon the calm air.

All day I had heard him singing thousands of songs of two to four, seldom five, notes. Monotonous, repetitious, preacher-like? His singing was all of this – if a recitation that was so intrinsic a phase of a creature's character, so innate an expression of self, could be any of these attributes.

Lovely and clear, simple and eloquent, his songs and intonations continued to reach me from the top of the aspen.

Hitherto his voice had been unaffected by his day-long singing. But now, as if he had reached the end and only with reluctance gave in, his songs shortened and were often just softly whispered. Then the sun hid behind alto-cumulus and it grew dusky in the vireo territory while out yonder, at the edge of the forest, the sun still threw its gold upon the trees and the hillsides.

Between 6:00 and 6:13 p.m. my vireo sang 44 songs. Two minutes later, with wings closed, he dropped from the crown of the aspen into a thick stand of young evergreens. From there, like an echo of his day's performance, he gave six more songs. Then he fell silent and was heard no more. Officially, the sun set one hour and 39 minutes later.

Fourteen hours, less six minutes, my red-eyed vireo had been awake. Of this time he spent nearly 10 hours singing a total of 22,197 songs. This was his record. But the most important is not the record, but my introduction to an individual bird and the glimpse he gave me of his true character.

At the end of the nesting period, when the young are being fledged or have already left the nest, a curiously relevant resurgence of courtship behaviour occurs between the parent birds – nature's reminder of its unyielding continuity. Song, this meaningful part of a bird's reproductive period, is also revived. So, at this time, the thrushes' vocal performances come into their own as never before. At dawn, and sometimes also in the evening, in the fullness of summer these birds fill the twilight intervals between day and night with their most inspired music, full-toned and lingering. Other birds already off tone, induced by the thrushes' example, may suddenly provide an accompaniment of sorts. This late-season singing by the thrushes and others sometimes lasts to the end of July, even into August, producing dawn concerts only the early riser will hear – never to forget.

The Walk at Dawn

John Burroughs, the famous American naturalist, once said: "To learn something new take the path you took yesterday!" So each morning at dawn I walked the familiar rocky path winding through the forest.

Dawn is the magic hour – I have said so before and I say it again. When the first reflections of the returning sun slowly tint the sky and landscape with the blushing colours of the air's humidity, then the environment emerges pure. The sins of the other day are washed away and the terrors of the night vanish.

Time has wrought great changes in this coniferous forest since we established our home 40 years ago upon a rocky hill along the shore of Pimisi Bay. And also in us.

Then the evergreens were young. The scarry blisters that later were to bleed so many of their tops dry did not yet show on the trunks of the white pines. Birches, aspens, and ashes stood side by side with young balsam firs like fresh adolescents, stretching eagerly for their places in the light. Others, only saplings but nevertheless useful, served many woodland song-birds that prefer the middle storey of the sylvan growth as a place in which to build their nests. During this earlier period the light penetrated through the sparser canopy down to the forest floor, encouraging a luxurious sprouting of soft maples, hazel, and the many-specied honeysuckles, prime fodder for the deer.

In those years the break of day was a time of intense avian exuberance. Dawn was the hour when the lingering cadences of the night singers, whippoorwills, thrushes, the ubiquitous spring peepers, reluctantly hushed or were drowned in the unison of the awakened day singers. Aroused by the light of the new day that seeped like a tide of illumination through the trees, voice was added to voice as the dawn chorus gained in volume minute by minute. The competition between the song-birds was keen; there were so many of them. And the heterogeneous harmonies of nature's less complex sounds mingled with the bird song – the splashing of a cow moose in the lily pads, the explosive crack of a twig, cause unknown, the soft, soft swishing noises of the rising morning breeze in the crowns of the pines.

But all this has changed. Now the evergreens stand broad and secure on vastly extended root systems, their variously spiked or richly feathered crowns 50 or 60 feet against the blueing sky, forming a vaulted roof full of skylights. As a result of the increased shade, many of the erstwhile thriving shrubs are gone, or they are markedly thinned out. The few soft maples that still insist upon competing with the trees do so by untypically extending their gaunt, absurdly weak-looking stems. Here and there new shoots sprout from old immortal roots, sparsely but stubbornly clothing in verdure some of the open spaces above a thick ground cover of shade-tolerant asters, bracken, crawling linnaeas, and polished wintergreens. And I walk with feet more searching for solid footing than before and with a cane to steady my step over protruding obstacles.

Having in other years rejoiced in the fullness and wealth of these natural surroundings with their abundant wildlife and lush vegetation, I could not avoid feelings of nostalgia at the loss of an earlier paradise. Until I engaged in these walks over the same path trodden a thousand times before, across the same roots, the same rocks, to the top of the rise of the land, then down past the spring where water bubbles from the earth clear as crystal, and through the humid dell covered with ferns to the main path.

It was springtime. Undisturbed and unemphasized, the deep silence of the dawn rang noiselessly in my ears. I listened with taut expectancy for some of the familiar voices that once filled the air. But there was no sound. Nothing. Occasionally I heard a drop of water hit an upturned leaf with a hollow sound. Then another, and then one drop fell from an oversaturated shelf down upon the spread fan of a bracken leaf with a hardly audible splash. Surprising! The sky was clear and no rain was falling. Where did the water come from? I listened intently. Suddenly, I knew. This was the dew falling, a sound impossible to detect except in a solid silence where no birds were singing, no twigs were cracking, no wind was moving. The dew, the eternal freshener, belonged to the dawn, having its magic effect upon the renewal of the day. Vapour condensed during the cool of the night, tiny drops fetched from the air to take shape, to adhere to each other, and to fall, a vital part of the global hydrological cycle.

Mid-July. Gradually the light stole in amongst the shadowy trees. Cool, selectively intoned notes came through the still air, so softly that on a spring day full of vivacity they would have been inaudible at that distance. But now the short introductory note was followed by a sequence of ascending notes, so deliberate in their delivery they seemed to be floating independently, dissociated from the singer. The beautifully modulated notes rose to a dizzy, almost sibilant high register and were there suspended. Until, presently, the first single note reintroduced the same theme.

After arrival in late April, the hermit thrush might announce with song for a few days his presence on a piece of land where he is not inclined to welcome others except a partner of his own kind. But once she appears, he becomes silent. The pressures of increasing domestic duties, centred around a nest secreted under low cover on the ground, gradually submerge all conspicuous behaviour. When the young are finally fledged and the stresses of family raising relaxed, a faint recrudescence of sexuality occurs within the birds. Latent tendencies toward renewed courtship are awakened for a short time, until the yearly moult sets in, and lure the hermit thrush to indulge in his most lyrical singing. And not only do these songs express peaceful relaxation but also a subdued glow, an esoteric animation, symbolizing the perpetuity of nature's reproductive cycles.

Presently, in the dissipating dusk, I caught a glimpse of the singer. With a graceful, slightly theatrical lift of the reddish tail, the thrush edged sideways along the branch. He started another song, slow, easy in performance, exquisitely euphonic under the vaulted roof of the forest. And the sun, about to slip across the edge of the eastern horizon, sent advance beams to tint delicately pink the morning mists. The thrush fell silent.

A tall bushy spruce of advanced age stands slightly southeast of my path. Its voluminous branches are rough from hoary ripeness and exposure. Its erect top peaks above the tallest of the pines. Evergreens of varied ages make up its entourage. On the ground a clump of trailing arbutus was just coming into bloom, and here and there delicately sculptured shoots of pink lady's-slippers penetrated the soft mat of green moss, intending to bloom in June.

One day in early May a tiny but brisk kinglet found its way into this benign habitat, his erected red crown spot shining like a ruby. Suitable elevation was here to be found, whence territorial singing by a small bird commanded excellent audibility, as well as fine sites for a nest to be tucked into the short pinlike leaves of the spruce's feathery branches. What more could a ruby-crowned kinglet require – except a mate with whom to share all this!

Having firmly established his claim on the land against all comers of his own species by almost uninterrupted singing, the kinglet continued to sing from sunrise to sunset. When these vocal efforts failed to attract a partner, one might have thought the bird would leave to seek a more promising location. But such was not the case.

Instead, the kinglet remained, regaling the neighbourhood with songs of such fine quality as I have seldom heard from a tiny greenish bird that moves inconspicuously among the somber conifers. The kinglet let one rippling song follow upon the other the whole day long, almost without cessation. Loud, rounded, amazingly full-toned for so tiny a singer, his notes fell leisurely, unhurried, almost languidly upon the air. And we, working, walking around the premises, living in the house with all the windows open, existed for weeks on end to the accompaniment of the kinglet's lovely rich motif. Our minds and senses absorbed it half unconsciously, unquestioningly, like those who love and understand good music absorb and take for granted the intricate composition of a favourite symphony. So inseparable a part of us did the bird's uninterrupted daily singing become that its cessation seemed implausible.

Then one sunrise – two months, less five days, after the ruby-crowned kinglet sang his first song – he gave two songs. The seemingly total silence that followed made our green world appear singularly empty.

Time wore on into August. At dawn the wood thrush was still singing. How long would he continue to sing? At the first break of day he sang more varied, softly syncopated phrases than at any other time of the day or the year. Sometimes he accelerated the tempo to produce an effect as though two birds were singing a duet, so rapidly did each phrase follow upon the other. And to a white-throated sparrow and an ovenbird, whose singing should long since have been silenced, the thrush's performance was of such enthralment that they invariably sang, irresistibly enticed into competition with these extraordinarily seductive recitals.

Presently the sun, preparing to rise, let a faint carmine tint play upon the trees. This was the signal. The thrush hushed, leaving only the white-throated sparrow to intone, as an echo, one solo song, clear as the sound of purling spring water.

The rim of the sun's blazing face welled like molten gold above the horizon. A liberated beam emblazoned with rosy red

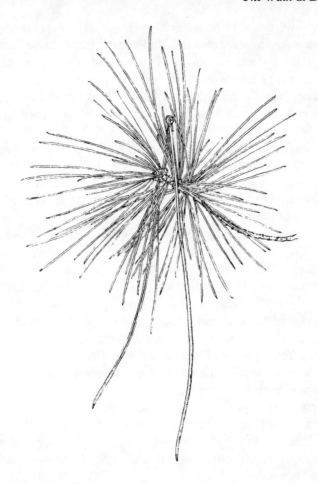

the trunk of a white birch in front of me and brought into bold relief the uneven pattern of its tattered bark.

August 6. A suggestion of coming light faintly outlined the eastern horizon. Suddenly, the wood thrush broke the deep silence with one single song, softly trailing, so brief, so isolated, that I doubted having heard it. By the path a red squirrel exploded in a loud querulous tirade to protest some unspecified annoyance. This, in turn, rudely awakened several small birds roosting with bills tucked under their scapulars and set off a chorus of chipping alarm notes. At the top of the path, without warning, I found myself in the midst of a throng of invisible outraged inhabitants. The whole wood thrush family was among them, one in front of me, *chet-tet-tet*, another over there, *chet-tet-tet*, and a third one so close behind me that as I stood motionless I heard the faint sound of its claws gripping the twig, of the air sifting through its feathers as it recovered a moment's lost balance. An animated exchange of soft calls bounced lightly from bird to bird and, listening, I could follow every move they made.

Far back, a red-eyed vireo gave a succession of tone poems, cut short now that fall was approaching. Chirring loudly, the squirrel ran off on its own errand. I held my breath, waiting for another sound, another song. But the magic moment of the forest's first awakening was past.

Throughout June the solitary vireos behaved so inconspicuously that when on occasion I caught a glimpse of their sleek olive-green forms, lovely with the bluish head, the white "spectacles" and bars on the wings, it was a warming surprise to find them still present. The solitary vireo is not a common bird even in these forests where it belongs. Associated with evergreens, for breeding purposes the bird seeks a spot where these darker trees stand intermixed with deciduous growth to create a lighter environment. And its colouring and its essence blend well with this background.

Then there was the song. Never until these late summer days had I fully appreciated the quality of the solitary vireo's song. It recalled the red-eyed vireo's broken phrasings but was slower, more full-toned and mellifluous, with some notes slightly slurred.

Proof of the pair's successful nesting came on July 3. Then, before my delighted eyes, a fledgling just out of the nest and its father's exact image revealed itself, securely perched on a rough twig in an old pine. The father approached it and, between songs of felicitous suasion, which caused the youngster almost to topple from its perch in its eagerness, fed it.

Thereafter followed several weeks during which the solitary vireo reached a peak of vocal performance. His singing was never profuse and always selectively timed between sunrise and the early forenoon. One might surmise that in the solitary vireo, as in the thrushes, a short period of sexual recrudescence inspires this singular late summer musicality. The highlight came one morning just after sunrise when, with the fragrance of warming conifers strong in my nostrils, I stood spellbound, listening to the exquisite notes of a chance duet. It was the solitary vireo giving his full, emphatic, slightly slurred phrasings, blending beautifully with the loud full-length warbling song of a purple finch. An occasion rare as violets blooming in snow, a moment brief as the fall of a raindrop, never again to be repeated.

Toward the end of August the solitary vireo's singing gradually subsided, and only the passing of migrants through his territory occasionally stirred him to vocal response. On September 3, just after sunrise, I heard the vireo sing once. After that, summer floated into the silences and emptiness of the year's fall.

Part Four

The Blooded Tooth and Nail

I have seen it happen so many times. It is difficult to avoid emotional involvement and to reconcile the event of death in nature with one's own preconceived ideas.

From out of nowhere the sleek fast sharp-shinned hawk dashes into the feeding-station area. In one single forceful charge it bears down upon the grey jay – a large prey for a small hunter. Strong talons closing quickly give scant room for the last breath. The next instant, the grey jay's slender body, rolled tightly into its flattened – once so fluffy – feathers, is being carried quickly out of sight. Later I find the rock where, according to the habit of the short-winged hawks, the raptor sat plucking its victim before tearing it asunder. How deeply had the familiarities of the peopled environment, the false security of the feeders, blunted the jay's wildness and robbed it of its natural alertness to let itself be so easily surprised by the hawk's smart manoeuvre?

Another picture comes to mind. This time a goshawk, the largest of the short-winged hawks, rose precipitously as I came upon it from a deep hollow in the soft snow with a dead ruffed grouse in its talons. The grouse had died quickly under the suffocating assault. The hawk's stiff wing pinions rustled as it laboriously flew off with the heavy prey weighing down its powerful lift. All that is left to tell the tale is a ring of downy feathers in the snow, streaked and patterned in the delicate design of the wood-brown, beige and black of the ruffed grouse.

Notoriously inoffensive, the snowshoe, or varying hare is the principal prey of many meat-eaters. Feeding on grass and other green plants during the warmer season, it survives during the winter by gnawing the bark of recent deciduous windfalls, shrubs and young trees. Often, the severity of the winter may be gauged by such encirclements at snow-height of the young trees' trunks.

The hare is a regular visitor at the feeding-station. So also, more seldom, is the pine marten. This far-ranging beautifully furred animal of the weasel family, with its pert triangular face and keen piercing eyes above the softly beige-coloured chest, is a highly dangerous commuter to the feeding areas frequented by the smaller beasts, the red squirrels and the snowshoe hares.

So one late afternoon, the hare, according to habit, meanders out of cover to feed peacefully on the open lawn's lush green grass and to look for a melon rind perchance thrown out around the feeder. This, ordinarily, was a perfectly safe place to be out in the open. The hare had not seen the marten stationed behind the rock fence, not more than three yards away. Nor was the marten aware of the presence of the hare. But as the marten emerged, the sight of the hare within easy grasp caused it to "freeze," mesmerized. The hare, whose eyesight is poor, does not see the marten. But a whiff of scent reaches its twitching nose. Reaction is instantaneous. At the same second as the marten crouches and springs, the hare's lightning turn, marvellously projected into incredible speed, just saves it from the marten's fatal throat grip. The powerful, lithe, fast marten stops almost before the chase starts, as if sensing it has met its match in agility.

If predation by far most vividly colours our ideas of the relations between predator and prey, birds and beasts, this is chiefly because of the dramatic suddenness and impact with which action usually takes place. It is, moreover, due to the very rare occasions when the much less dramatic non-predatory encounters between them come to the watcher's notice. The truth is, of course, that predation happens only under special circumstances, when a combination of timely facts, such as hunger, the situation, the time of day or season, combine to make it inevitable. Peaceful and at times quite profitable meetings between birds and other animals do take place, far more often than the watcher is usually allowed to witness.

So it was one day when I caught the yellow-bellied sapsucker in the trap attached to the tree-trunk. At the touch of my hand the bird voiced piercing screams. Sitting invisible under the thick bracken, the snowshoe hare heard the screams, dashed into the open and tore madly around my legs, whining softly, excitedly, in response to the woodpecker's screams.

Obviously, mistaking the bird's screams for the distress cry of its leveret born not long ago, the hare flung caution to the winds and rushed out of cover to its rescue. But there was no leveret. A vastly different situation prevailed. Confused, the hare ran around in circles, searching for the leveret until, finally, the bird's screams subsided. The incentive having thus evaporated, the hare, still whining softly, retreated under the protecting shelter of the bracken.

Family worries and the annual moult all over by early October, the female ruffed grouse walks sedately across the lawn into the lightly frost-bitten flower-bed. She is a bird in the grey-phase plumage, the red-phased ones being rare around Pimisi Bay. Her thin black ruff lies flat against her neck and her grey tail with its broad broken black band is folded tight together like a drawing rule.

A chipmunk, on a like leisurely autumn stroll before going

into its winter sleep, runs up to the grouse, whose shadow swamps it. The chipmunk stops just short of collision, sniffs the air with a knowing look upon its pointed physiognomy. The rash advance of the small animal intimidates the grouse. She side-steps, opens her fan of a tail, tilts it at the same time as the black ruff rises to frame her small beaked face. The bird raises, balloons the feathers on her breast and flanks, loosens her wings from her flanks, and thus presents her tiny antagonist with an imposing giant-sized image. Undismayed, the chipmunk dismisses the overwhelming sight, finds nothing else to satisfy its curiosity and runs off, leaving the big bird standing there in all its pomposity of dress and pose without a target.

The problem of predation is not easy to accept unquestioningly, especially when the predatory transgressions of our own species weigh so heavily in the environmental balance. But in the larger patterns of nature a principle seems to have evolved whereby a fine line is drawn between the predator and the prey, setting certain limits. Not too many, and not too few. John Muir, the noted naturalist, put it this way: "A predator's ability to catch its prey must balance with the prey's ability to escape." The predator is thus allowed a certain range of determinate chances contrived, in part, by circumstances and, partly, by its own acquired skills. In response, the prey also develops aptitudes, such as vigilance, being in a constant state of *qui vive*, as well as a remarkable capacity for instantaneous reaction – such as in the case of the hare's narrow escape from the marten – enabling it to overcome, to a degree, the risks set upon its path against its survival. Directly or indirectly, predator and prey serve as controls upon each other. Grasped or neglected, the split-second chance to live or to die, to catch or to miss, is the main issue and the impulse that keeps the pendulum swinging toward the optimum balance between the survival rates of both.

In the Afternoon of a Fawn

It was a brilliant morning in March. The sun blazed down upon Pimisi Bay and on the Mattawa River. The high vertical cliffs on either side of the river reflected the sunlight and its glorious warmth. Below Talon Chute the water lay open and smoking. But on the lake the ice was hard and granulated from the effects of deep-freezing nights and daytime sun-thaw, and it gave off translucent heat waves visible only against the distance.

All of a sudden, a deer leapt out in front of me from behind the point. Bouncing high as if made of nothing but air and rubber, it bounded over the ice, flag aloft, showing the long silky hairs underneath flounced into a magnificent white rosette. A smart crunchy tattoo with a hollow undertone resounded from the ice under the deer's hoofs.

The deer stopped, all four legs spread disorderly in the pose of the last interrupted motion. With irrepressible curiosity, it looked around at me, who had disturbed its lazy browsing in the sunshine. Then up went its head in a movement of playful defiance, and it set off in a parade trot, the like of which was never equalled in the highest equestrian school.

Hoofs scarcely touching the ice in the high-stepping gait, the deer flung wide its forelegs in elaborate semi-circles, and swung its graceful head from side to side in a high mood of extravagance and show, born, surely, of the life-giving brilliance of the sun. Never has any choreographer designed a *pas seul*, or a Nijinsky executed a measure, of more plastic perfection than the dance over the sparkling ice of this wild and free fawn. There was no negative element in this show of motion, no fright in the speed, nor desire to be gone out of sight. Here was all the pithy reality of pure exuberance, of pure beauty, set against a backdrop of ice and sky and wooded shoreline, a natural performance such as no stage has ever

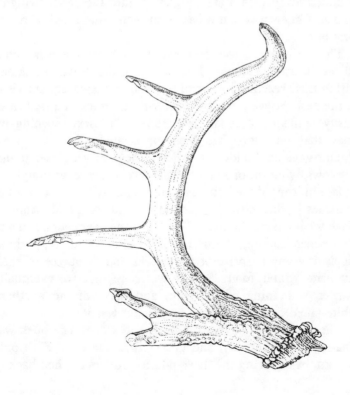

witnessed. For minutes I stood watching in spellbound delight, until the hoof-beats died away and the deer vanished behind wreaths of rising vapours at the First Rapids.

A winter and a half passed from the time the deer first arrived in our territory until we saw them. In all this time, we read the fresh evidence of their presence nearly every day in the marks left by their dainty hoofs as they stepped along our paths, or made four-footed take-offs into the soft snow, or stamped around amid the white cedar brush on the terrace below the house overlooking Pimisi Bay. So close they had been under our windows, yet never seen. Elusive, they were like mirages, forever vanishing, discrediting even the signs of their own passing.

Then, on the second day of the new year, it happened. Well-nigh a hundred times I had come outside stealthily, trusting to luck that some day I would surprise these shy animals. But this day I forgot. Scared by my sudden appearance, a deer bounded away with a startling snort into the dawn twilight. And all I knew was that it had been there, that I had seen it at long last.

The spot where the deer had been browsing was about 50 feet from the house. Hardly any cedar leaves remained within their reach in the small grove after their frequent visits in the past. So we put a block of salt on a rock and tied fresh bushy branches of cedar to a trunk. The next morning we knew that our efforts had been appreciated.

This gave us the idea of enticing the deer yet closer to our windows by means of a gradual advance of the cedar boughs to a place in front of the house, where we planted a small forest of branches in the snow. We moved the salt, too, and cleared a place for it beside the path. Very soon the deer caught on and they began coming to this feeding bower regularly, without displaying any surprise at the everlasting resources of their favourite winter food. And it was here that we eventually learned something of the ways and plays of the northern white-tailed deer, *Odocoileus virginianus borealis*.

There were two of them, a buck and a doe. The buck was small, young probably, and greyer than the doe. With only tiny knobs replacing the three-pointed antlers he shed back of the house last fall, he looked like the doe's fawn. His large liquid eyes were fringed with long curved lashes and gazed upon the world with trusting naïveté. He stepped daintily as if on limber stilts and the spread of his cloven hoofprint revealed his mood and the speed of his advance. Nearly always he took the lead ahead of the doe in an apologetic way, as if her safe conduct were his chief concern. Even when she was out of sight, his constant and acute consciousness of her whereabouts was never in doubt. He kept throwing back his head over his shoulder, his munching jaws still and his eyes fixed in the direction from whence, sure enough, she eventually emerged to pose like a figure carved on the brow of the hill.

In shape and temperament the essence of fleetness, the deer in repose and safety, as I was to learn in time, were past masters of slow-motion. The doe took exactly 20 minutes to descend from the brow of the hill to the feeding place at the window, a distance of a scant 150 feet. Her large ears twitching nervously, she came down with extreme cautiousness, stepping as if on pins.

She withdrew and set down her hoofs, one at a time, precisely in the buck's tracks, and without disturbing a speck of snow or leaving an additional light mark of her own slender shins. She took advantage of every bit of cover provided by naked bushes that stuck out of the snow or by the lower branches of the evergreens, behind which the outline of this large and deliberate animal became so confused as to render her all but invisible. On bright, moonlit nights, when the interplay of silvery light and blue-black shadows created fantastic patterns upon the snow-covered forest floor, I saw her retire into an obscure patch and become totally engulfed by it in all her ruminant amplitude, as if she were no longer there.

I knew the doe from the buck anywhere because she was curiously unlike him. She was of a lighter fawn colour and her head was more elongated than his. An odd kind of dignity and maturity characterized her poses and movements; her girth was ample and her flanks spacious and she lacked only the fawn at her side to complete the maternal mammalian picture. Oftentimes she merely stood, interminably, wearing a vastly bored expression and chewing the cud thoroughly and endlessly.

After she got his "all-safe" signal, she took no further notice of the buck. Only on occasion, when the two met at close range, she displayed recognition that they belonged together. She would throw up her head and snap at him, and sometimes she reared against him with pawing forefeet and ears flipped back flat as if annoyed at his proximity. But how could I guess her feelings?

Their approach to the feeding place was a matter of grave importance, since it involved the security of an existence perhaps more vulnerable and precarious than that of any other sylvan inhabitant. They used two main avenues, down the steep incline from the brow of the hill or along the path from the spring. Both these approaches had the advantage of enabling them to survey the feeding place and its surroundings spread out below without themselves being seen, before they emerged from behind a curtain of evergreen branches. Often they stood there for half an hour or more, as if to outwait any chance disturbance, before they decided to come down at last. But when, during a number of visits, the place proved to be devoid of upsetting elements, the deer rapidly became accustomed to the peacefulness of the situation and began moving about with greater confidence.

Yet, even as they stood munching the cedar boughs below our window, every muscle and nerve of their bodies was constantly aquiver. A leaf rustled, a chickadee twittered, and the deer's ears flicked, always on the *qui vive*. When the wind in the pine above dumped a pad of snow on the roof with a thud, the little buck sank to his knees in a spontaneous motion of avoidance. But the conditioning of the deer to the cars, trucks and buses that rumbled, roared and backfired, racing up and down the hill on the highway only a few hundred feet away, was of long standing. Provided none stopped, provided no other sound was mixed with their noise, such as the clatter of a horse's hoofs or the crunching of a man's soles against the pavement, and that no unfamiliar movement could be detected except that of the speeding vehicles, the deer treated them as air. Not even did the animals shy away from them during a playful canter in the moonlight; instead the prancing deer often danced alongside these roaring monsters with their glaring eyes as if they belonged to the play.

Our faces in the window were a source of apprehension to the doe especially. Were they there before she arrived, she appeared oblivious of them until a movement gave them away. Then she bounded off. But she soon returned, trying out various new approaches, watching the window intently, until she was apparently reassured that either the faces did not see her or she could no longer see them. At other times she stood her ground and gazed upon the "odd" apparitions, raising and lowering her head as if to make sure her eyes did not deceive her. But in due time, the faces in the window, like the cars on the road, were accepted as harmless and inescapable accessories to this particular environment. For the deer's own safety, this was as far as we wished to pursue their taming.

At that time the house harboured a cat which, quite naturally, considered the surroundings as his territory and the deer as illegitimate trespassers. He made this known by racing up a tree-trunk, tail fluffed and claws noisily scratching the bark; or he jumped on the roof and galloped around, finally pretending to spring upon the heads of the jittery deer but saving himself by a hair's breadth. The deer fled. But soon they gained courage, since this toy panther apparently lacked both the size and attributes that to them meant danger. One night, as the cat commenced his intimidation routines, the buck faced him in front of the doe. With tails lifted and the long white hairs of their flags spread and stiffened the deer met threat with threat; the buck gave an explosive snort and with a motion almost too pretty to convey belligerency he stamped the ground three times with his dainty front hoofs. The effect of these moves upon the cat was spectacular and all further demonstrations on its part were inhibited.

This was what we saw of the deer at the feeding place. They came there at all times, at dawn and at dusk, in the dark of the night and in the bright light of midday; but most often they came in the afternoon. Often they came in snowy weather with their backs, shoulders, and long eyelashes powdered white. Only on cold days, when the thermometer dipped below zero, they stayed away, sometimes for several days. Those days they took shelter back in the woods under the spruces and balsam firs, whose lower branches were caught in the deep snows and formed snug circular tents around the trunks. There, underneath, the snow was tramped hard by the deer's hoofs. It was here, too, that I sometimes surprised them bedded down in the snow, once the two together just beyond the brow of the hill, but more often a little apart, and always on a small elevation with a view commanding the surrounding country. Almost before I saw them, they were gone, arisen on knees and hing legs in one motion, to cast themselves off and away in a giant first leap. And only the steaming hollow where they had lain, scooped out by their body heat, remained to tell that they had really been there.

One day, blood-curdling yelpings cut sharply and grimly through the dawn silence. The next instant a deer in a wild panic crashed through branches and bushes down the slop in front of the house. Another raced across the spring and took the highway like a broad ditch almost without the touch of a hoof. I got my snowshoes on fast and ran back into the woods to see what was happening. And there in the snow and in the gathering light I pieced together the story of that dawn.

That morning the timber wolves whose five and one-half inch tracks I had measured on the lake only a short while ago had their day among the deer back of the house. I saw where one wolf had come upon the standing deer and sent them racing for their lives in all directions. I saw the evidence of tight pursuit between cloven hoofs and padded feet. I followed it and some time later I came upon the end far out on High Point.

It was all over, all finished. Death feeds upon life and life upon death, and this is the law. Only two deer were down, one, then a little further on another, hamstrung, then stumbling and falling in their tracks. For many a day a few wolves and at least one fox fed undisturbed and well upon these two and sought no other prey. When they had finished, there was nothing left, save tufts of hairs scattered about for the birds to use in their nests, come springtime. There was no carnage. If left to herself nature does clean work, and seldom exacts the penalty of prolonged suffering.

The snow was gone and the sun beat down upon the warming fragrant earth. On a sunny slope I saw two deer. One of them threw up his head and looked at me as if recognizing something it was used to seeing, then continued his browsing. I could not mistake that doe nor the little grey buck escorting her. And, inconsequent as our affections make us, I could not suppress my relief knowing that just these two were the ones which escaped that fateful dawn.

The following winter only the doe returned to the feeding place she remembered, but she was not alone. Two small bucks accompanied her. They had lost their spots but by looks and behaviour clearly marked themselves as none other than the doe's twin fawns born early last spring.

In the forested areas, wherever the undergrowth provides good browse and nature's well-balanced cycles persist, the story of the white-tailed deer continues into summer and fall, into other winters and spring. Increasing humanity encroaches ever more severely on the available habitats suitable for these larger ruminants. When in any given area conditions suddenly come to a head, crises evolve. Inevitably, the deer population adjusts to the reduced size of the available room required for the survival of these larger animals.

In a secluded spot among the bushy young spruces of a growing forest a collection of soft deer hairs lie in a hollow. Here a deer died. Perhaps it was wounded by a hunter's gun; or the deep snow of the past severe winter prevented it from moving around sufficiently to secure enough fodder to satisfy its hunger. Not so long ago, the end was enacted, leaving no vestige save the hairs of the living creature. From the tall red cliff by the river, another deer, pursued by wolves in a wild chase, leapt, plunged to its death. The wolves dragged the body out on the ice, and half a dozen of them, several foxes and a flock of ravens drew sustenance from it and survived. For there is no loss, no end, only change, and all shall profit thereby.

Thus They Shall Perish

A muffled scream, the sharp snapping sound of wings whipping against the nesting branch, and the swift retreat of a trim falcon out over the lake; this was all I heard and saw of the tragedy.

Up there, high in the top of the white pine that stood overshadowing the house at Pimisi Bay, was the nest of a Blackburnian warbler. I had watched it ever since the day when the pretty female, dressed in "black and white and a dash of orange," had been busy finishing off the nest with a lining of fine rootlets and long hairs. I had watched it during 12 days of incubation, always with a feeling of anxiety lest a red squirrel should discover it while cutting down the cones that hung in heavy gummy clusters around it. But I never thought of the pigeon hawk.

When the young hatched I could not see them, but I

envisioned the half-transparent, half-naked blind nestlings opening yellow-pinkish cavities towards their parents, as with airy swoops the bright-coloured warblers alighted on the branch, shaking it a little. The female still brooded the young for long periods to keep them warm or to shield them from too much sunshine. But the rate of their feedings was increasing as the young grew and throve on their wormy diet.

The birds were five days old when, on a bright and warm summer morning, the mother bird went foraging in the red pine nearby. The sight of thousands of swarming May flies, sticking to pine needles and twigs wherever they found footing, had brought her out of the nest and she filled her crop with them. With her bill full she swung back toward the nest over the short distance that separated the red and the white pine trees.

Then it happened. In a split second the deed was done, timed so perfectly that the little bird neither heard nor saw death coming upon her on sharp-pointed wings. At first I did not realize what had happened. It had been too swift, too momentous, too mortal.

What would happen next? What were the chances of survival of those motherless ones up there in the pine-top? The male continued to come and go, following his accustomed and ordained rhythm of feeding and foraging. Would his instinct tell him of the emergency, whisper to him of the necessity to brood, to warm his nestful of offspring now that the female was no longer there to do it?

That afternoon it began to rain. Great heavy drops of cooling water fell and broke with a splash and a humid fog hung about the pine-tops. Every time I looked, the nest was unprotected. I shuddered thinking of the deathly chill that enveloped those birdlings. Time and again I awoke during the night, hearing the rain pouring down incessantly over the woods. Vehemently, I reproached nature for instructing the dead mother to build her nest so far up out of my reach that I could not save her young.

The next morning the male continued to visit the nest to feed one, perhaps two, nestlings that were still alive. He came and went, true to the duties that were his. He sang more beautifully and consistently than I had heard him sing for many days.

Finally, there was no opened bill to greet him. But to birds facts are not proved by reason but by endless repetition of circumstances. He left the nest and returned again. This time he pushed a meal into one yellow-pink cavity that weakly lifted itself toward him. After that, more and more often, he was obliged to eat the food he brought for the weakening nestlings. When, at last, they no longer accepted his offerings, his visits became rarer. Finally, he flew away for the last time, and song after song burst from his quivering throat.

I felt better when I knew that all of the young ones were dead. Their dying must have been easy and merciful, perhaps they just fell asleep never to awaken. It was only to me, mortal human, that the inexorable fate falling upon them appeared so heart-breaking.

Then the thought came to me: before I passed judgement upon the murderer, before I decided what was right and what was wrong, I must learn more about the pigeon hawk. For somewhere, hidden deeply within the fundamental laws of nature, I felt there must exist an explanation, a rightfulness, a logical co-ordination of life and death, that would relieve my feelings of the sense of cruelty and perhaps even justify the hawk's killing of the female warbler.

On the east side of Brulé Hill, in the tallest white pine, I found the pigeon hawk. A scorching fire had swept over the hill 14 years before and left a regiment of charred pine tree skeletons pointing skywards from its crest. The female sat on a stick nest securely supported by stout branches against the trunk of the tree.

At that moment she struck me as the most beautiful creature nature ever created. What poise, what bearing, what grace of outline! Her colour was dark, dark brown with a slaty shine when a sunray played upon her back. Her long tail, held at an angle over the rim of the nest, suggested broad bands of darker and lighter brown. On her breast the ground colour of her body lightened to creamy buff with bold dark stripes creating a striking pattern. Her hooked beak, toothed on each side, gave her an air of nobility. Over her shining eye, nature had penciled a fine light line, enhancing the clarity, the depth and far-sightedness of her wide steady gaze. In all the time of our acquaintance, through the vicissitudes of our hostility to forbearance and understanding, my impression of her beauty never lessened. Beautiful she was, whatever she did, from the beginning unto the end.

Behind, on the crest of the hill, perched motionless in the top of a burned-out pine, the male observed my approach with sphinx-like solemnity. He was smaller than she, a fraction lighter in colour. A stiff easterly wind swept up the hillside and over the crest and ruffled the feathers of the bird. He sat unmoved.

The female bobbed her head, perhaps to impress me, strange and unwanted intruder, with her animosity. Suddenly she arose and her long cream-coloured pantaloons, with their tear-drop markings, revealed her strong yellow legs and talons. She began to scream, sharply, loudly, *keeyickyickyick-yick*, a farflung, strident protest against the violation of her inherent right of seclusion. The male, lowering his head between his shoulders and lifting his trim wings, answered her.

She took off. And then both birds began an aerial display, the like of which I had never seen. Borne on the high wind, lifted by the up-currents of air and riding the downdraughts, caught abreast by unexpected gusts of wind, which made them turn, wheel, glide through the trees at incredible angles with fantastic speed and agility, they swept and circled in a dance of hostility down over me, up and above me. I stood breathless, listening to the rush of air through their wings as they swooped low over me, fascinated by the graceful motions of these two streamlined falcons, by their superb control of every law of flight governing an airborne body.

Suddenly this aerial war-dance ended. The male flew screaming out over the lake. The female, her yellow landing-gear braced, alighted squat on a pine-top that bent weakly under her weight. She bobbed her head, looked down upon me, then threw a glance toward her nest. She screamed, circled the nesting tree, then swooping down, alighted on the rim of the nest. With the same kind of protecting snuggling movement as any other brooding bird would display, she settled on her eggs.

The tree overlooked a sheltered bay of the lake that opened widely beyond to the north. One might have supposed that all the small birds would shun so dangerous a neighbourhood. But it was by no means a lifeless place. A yellow-green Nashville warbler sang from an exposed perch on his nesting grounds that actually overlapped the falcons' territory. Below, in the thicket, not a stone's throw from the hawks' nest, a veery, an olive-backed thrush, some Canada warblers, redstarts and yellow-throats had hidden their nests. On the west side, a pair of robins were feeding early young in their mud-lined home.

All of these birds sang, fed, and meandered around, often going right into the hawks' nesting tree, apparently in perfect safety. When sighting the hawks the small birds behaved exactly as they usually do when other birds come into their nesting territories. They would scold roundly, and even attack the birds of prey twice their own size. The robins, being under high tension at this stage of their nesting, would not tolerate the sight of the falcons. Once when the female hawk rested in the top of a burnt-out pine guarding the nest while the male was away, the two robins worried her like buzzing bees. Not 15 feet away from her they perched, scolding, and more than once they dove on the hawk, nearly unseating her. The falcon only shifted on her perch, bobbed her head and regarded her attackers with a piercing eye. Although the robins were well within the hawk territory and had not the slightest chance of escape had she moved to attack, never once did the hawk retaliate. Why, why? I asked myself. What a meal within reach of her talons! Was she not hungry? Why did she not avenge herself?

In the course of time the riddle was solved. These two hawks were never seen to hunt within their own territory and hence their neighbours lived with them in safety. The hawk boundary ran all around Brulé Hill, but beyond that line, the rules of the hunt were in force. The only time I saw the hawk break the safety zone convention was one day when a foolish young hairy woodpecker trespassed quite innocently. The female hawk had just finished feeding her young. She looked at the woodpecker, swiftly made up her mind and dashed after him. What a ride that woodpecker got! But there was nothing wrong with his instinctive reactions. He dodged around tree-trunks and, finally, saved himself in the thicket below the hill. Why the hawk broke the small-bird safety rule this time is difficult to explain. Was the trespasser too big to come under the small-bird category?

There was a size limit to the birds allowed free passage through the hawk domain and the falcons' behaviour toward larger birds, such as crows, and other hawks, changed altogether. One of these had but to show itself within half a mile and the hawk boundary leaped out to meet it. Then the small falcons streaked off to the attack with wild screams. That their beaks and talons were effective, the grunts and squawks of the pursued birds bore witness. The hawks attacked from above and sometimes from below, turning in mid-air with raking talons against the unprotected soft parts of the pursued, forcing their enemies to lift awkwardly to escape injury. They were invincible in their territorial defense. Not a bird was large enough to daunt them. With the great blue heron, they carried their intolerance almost to the ridiculous. That poor awkward giant with his slow wing-beat and long dangling legs, perfectly harmless, perfectly innocent of any predatory intent, was never permitted a peaceful frog luncheon in the sheltered bay below the nest. To see the male falcon, mosquito-like by comparison, taking long rides on the back of the squawking heron, was laughable.

During incubation and after the young falcons had hatched, the male did most of the hunting. He streaked through the trees, his head low between his shoulders. On past the nest he came, with his limp prey dangling from his talons. The female screamed her welcome, long before I saw him, and left the nest in pursuit. With acrobatic precision the transfer of the prey often took place in mid-air. Sometimes the male perched, held out the prey to his mate, and she took it from him on the wing. She plucked it and ate it hungrily in some burned-out pine. Later, when she was feeding the young, she took it to the nest and plucked it, sitting on the rim. Then she fed it to the nestlings piecemeal. After the hunt, the male rested for a long time, sometimes for hours, perched like an immobile statue in the top of a tree.

Mealtimes did not come often, twice or three times, perhaps four times a day when the young were hatched. There was no hunting between meals, not even when a tasty prize presented itself tantalizingly within reach. They ate when they were hungry, in order to live. I never saw them kill simply for the pleasure of killing.

In spite of his agility and masterly hunting talent, the pigeon hawk does not come by his living easily. He hunts by sight, quick dash, and surprise. His prey – insect, small rodent or bird – is small, wary, swift, and expert at dodging. I have seen a kingbird, conspicuous both in looks and behaviour and not a fast flier, elude him because of its presence of mind. I have seen the falcon shoot past a "frozen" white-throated sparrow, so obvious I could not believe the hawk could have missed it. The sporting odds in nature have been fairly divided between hunter and prey to the benefit of both.

Having thus studied and gradually discovered the characteristics of the pigeon hawks and their specific traits, my sympathies for them grew. I could not help but admire their devotion to family and to each other; their attitude of "live and let live" which seemed inviolate in their home territory; their apparent refusal to kill for sport, the revelation of which shall never again permit me to call them murderers. Nevertheless, when watching a luckless purple finch being plucked, its blood-stained feathers descending slowly upon a faint wind, or the innocent head of a scarlet tanager rolling on the ground beneath the perched falcon, or the young hawks fighting over a piece of gut belonging to a graceful thrush, I found it hard to suppress my emotion. It took me a long time to achieve a reconciliation of these two contradictory sides of nature.

And yet, to all the hawks' victims, death came swiftly, like a thunderbolt, with hardly an instant of pain or anguish. Never once did they bring in a bird that was not dead. The force with which they struck was evidently enough to kill and the grip of their talons suppressed the last quivering reflexes.

If death is inevitable to all nature's creatures, could it strike at a more glorious moment than at the height of an accelerated life cycle, as in the case of the warbler, whatever the consequences? Or could it interfere more mercifully than when an accident or disease spelled the oncoming of the irrevocable end for a maimed or ailing bird and slowed up its tempo? It is only in human thought that the life is all-important in itself, its essence neglected for the sake of its preservation.

And how can it be said truthfully that there is more rightfulness in a bird killing insects for the support of its life, than in the hawk's killing of the bird for the support of its own existence? Each one, as I now see it, is either as wrong or as right as the other. Which life, in the light of evolution and the future, has more significance than the other, that of the progeny of the warbler, or the hawk, or of any other species? Nature, in its perpetuity, recognizes no higher or lower forms but only the living as part of all life. No creature is exempt from dying. In nature one life is merely a part of a link in the everlasting chain of evolution.

Nor is it to be forgotten that if the pigeon hawk acts as a control upon the smaller bird populations to promote their strength and soundness as a living force, the hawks, in turn, are subject to exactly the same kind of control.

Among the enemies of the pigeon hawks are other hawks, crows and man. One day a crow alighted on the nest of the falcons and, had I not been there just at that moment, one or eventually all of the woolly hawklets doubtless would have served as a banquet for the crow. And then, as if to prove the immutable necessity of readjustment and counter-balance, misfortune befell the young hawks even as it did the young warblers. First the father hawk, then the mother disappeared, presumably having come to their end through man, the most inveterate slayer ever known.

But this time nature left the abandoned young birds in a more accessible place. I took them down and put them in an open nest cage from which two of them eventually departed safely. The inherent rights of the falcons, such as I had learned to understand them, supported this action of mine.

However difficult for us to admit the rightfulness of the victim as well as that of the predator, and to accept death not as an ending, but as an attribute of life, these opposing forces are part of the very essence of living. The sacrifice of life means the sustenance of animated power, for life exists and is nourished by life itself. In this there may be drama, but not tragedy.

Thus They Shall Survive

About half-way between the Great Lakes and the southern-most tip of James Bay lies the small lake, Pimisi Bay. Here in the ecotone between the deciduous forests of the south and the great evergreen forests of the north we have experienced not only the changes of the seasons, but based on our daily observations and records, we have also seen how the larger cyclic interrelated patterns in the life of the wilderness emerge from year to year, from decade to decade. The land possesses the magnificent harshness and austerity of the north. Its rounded sweeping contours evolved from the pre-Cambrian era to the present through the full scale of geological creation. Rivers, rapids, waterfalls, tall cliffs, and deep ravines cut through the forest. Since the severe harvesting of the virgin forests almost a century ago, the second-growth trees have re-established a maturing forest. In many places this new forest has reached a climax and stands there dark, tall, and dense, with scant underbrush. But in other places of recent cuts the evergreens are growing up young and vigorous, lightened by the succession of aspens, birches, and the soft maples.

In December, 1970, with the last lap of a wave hushed and still under the first brittle sheet of ice to cover the lake, winter came to Pimisi Bay. Eighty-seven days were to elapse thereafter before winter's grip would be loosened sufficiently once again to send the thermometer above the freezing point.

At Christmas the below-zero temperatures set in, and by the end of the year a foot of snow covered the ground. January went by with a glittering show of sharp crystal-clear weather that froze the breath on our faces and made the wood crack with sudden loud reports in the trees and in the house. The sharpest and longest spell of below-zero weather ushered in February with a promise of six more long weeks of winter. And then came the snow. One wild storm followed upon the other so closely as hardly to give birds and beasts and men a breathing spell. The snow whirled and drifted in through gaps in the forest open to the weather, coming to rest hard-packed in beautifully sculptured waves and swirls. Softly contoured mounds of snow accumulated on top of the very young evergreens and totally buried them. In the forest the snow lay 43 inches deep, a trackless cover insulating the ground against deeply penetrating frosts. The grouse buried itself deep down in the snow and slept there out of harm's way. The small mammals, the mice, shrews, and the red squirrels, opened a network of tunnelled traffic lanes under the snow.

It was late summer when the white pines gave me the first indication of interesting events to come. Their branches swayed and bowed under burdens of enormous clusters of redolent, closed green cones exuding drops of sticky resin that sparkled in the sun. In the past 23 years we had not seen the white pines with so rich a setting of cones. And the berry-bearing plants also displayed an abundance of fruit, some of which remained hanging on the branches throughout the winter, deep-frozen. The catkin aggregates of the white birches contained full stores of their minute, winged starlike nuts. Indeed, all over the forest an unusually generous supply of natural foods was in clear evidence. For the northern species of birds that do not, unlike the swallows and the warblers and all the others, subscribe to regular migrations south each fall, the abundance of natural foods plays an important role in directing or inhibiting their winter movements.

So, based on our records and earlier experience, I ventured a prediction: this winter we would have an invasion of finches, and the grey jays, the blue jays, the chickadees, and the nuthatches would be staying right here at home.

In late August the red squirrels were stressfully engaged in harvesting part of the coniferous wealth. Cones detached on high by the squirrels dropped like manna from heaven on paths, roofs, our heads, everywhere, with sharp sudden thuds. In short order the squirrels had every last one of their burrows filled to overflowing. With the mighty hoarding urge within them still unabated, they amassed mounds of cones outside the storehouses, rounds upon rounds of cones, all with their tips turned toward the centre. Fiercely the owner of each mound defended it against fellow intruders bent on petty thievings. Maddened, battling antagonists upset the tidy arrangements of the cones. Testily the owners rearranged them. And later in the winter, I was to find all over the forest untold heaps of discarded scales from cones hoarded by the resident squirrel, retrieved, and picked clean of their beautiful, winged twin seeds. Indeed, this was a winter of great beneficence for the red squirrel.

The blue jays were the first to fall in line with my winter forecast. I have proved to my own satisfaction by banding, and watchers have observed countless times, that our northern blue jays sometimes migrate south in the fall. This year they didn't. By mid-October they began congregating at the feeding-station at Pimisi Bay. Their numbers quickly reached a winter peak of about 40 to 50, compared with a year of migration when a dozen resident blue jays or less find sufficient supplementary support at the feeding-station to stay all winter. They visited the feeders in relay parties. Throw out a handful of bread – this was the order of the day – and the next instant a blue sea of jays milled over the bonanza. With bills propped helplessly agape by oversized loads of bread to be eaten or hoarded in privacy, the leaders managed to emit hoarse cries, a sort of come-hither note that evidently served to inform the others in the area of the food source found.

No evening grosbeaks nested at Pimisi Bay in the summer of 1970. But in November some appeared. During the fourth week they increased to a sizeable flock. All were males, illuminating the dark days with their showy and beautifully blended black, brown, yellow, and white plumages. Their powerful nutcracker bills were bone white. This told me nothing, for it is common practice for stray flocks of male evening grosbeaks to spend the winter in our latitudes.

Then a few females arrived. Modestly dove-grey, lightly washed with yellow, their black wings and rear accoutrements strewn with pearly white dots and suitably displayed in flight and posturings, they were alert and responsive to the exhilarating male companionship. This did provide me with an important clue. My records show that the presence here in winter of evening grosbeak females always coincides with inhibited southward migration. Very soon the steady increase in the numbers of evening grosbeaks at Pimisi Bay affirmed the suppression of any migration this winter. Laments from observers in the south reached me: Where are the evening grosbeaks?

This augured well for my prophesied "finchy" winter. So I began looking for the expected invasion along the roadsides where the salty slush thrown aside by snow-ploughs and cars always proves irresistible to the wintering finches. Sure enough, they came. Soon I found flocks of pine siskins, these inconspicuous, heavily striped little birds with their "buzzy" notes, sitting tight in some favoured place, darting away at my approach, only to swarm back to almost precisely the same delectable spot. And the goldfinches came, all in modest female dress. They alighted en masse on a patch of weed stalks sticking up and out of the snow. And there they sat, hugging the weed heads in intimate embrace until picked clean of seeds. They, too, relished the highway salt and grit. Then, a week or so later, came the purple finches. Tight-feathered, soft-voiced, companionable, as are most of the finches, the females and the immatures in their brownish-grey stripes outnumbered the fully coloured males, which were the first to let warbled notes proclaim the expectancy of spring.

If the presence of certain birds characterized certain patterns in the natural history of our forest, so also did the absence of some. That winter I would have been surprised to record an influx of pine grosbeaks and grey jays. Neither came. Both species are highly sedentary. The pine grosbeaks are well able and content to support themselves on the buds and seeds of the conifers and on frozen fruits, such as the red clusters of the staghorn sumac's cornlike stone fruits, and many others. And the grey jays, soft and fluffy in their inordinately long and highly insulating contour feathers, turn mainly meat-eater and scavenger in winter, and usually find ample opportunities to gorge on someone else's kill and other haphazard sources of animal remains. Only situations of excessive population densities and exhausted supplies of natural foods might drive flocks of pine grosbeaks and scattered grey jays out of their normal winter ranges in the northern forests in search of sufficient support.

However, two features in the occurrence of winter birds were definite aberrations from what might have been expected. One was the absence of the crossbills, both the red and the white-winged species. Neither had failed to appear during a similar invasion of winter finches in any previous year. There was nothing to explain their absence.

The other was the surprise arrival of one male slate-coloured junco and four tree sparrows. What caused their urge to fly south to evaporate at the Pimisi Bay latitude also remained unexplained.

True, normally migrating sparrows have been known to winter near feeding-stations much further north than Pimisi Bay. Only recently a junco, also a male, spent the winter here, perhaps the same bird; the fidelity of individual birds to their winter territory, as well as to their breeding area, is proven. Does this represent a trend whereby the limits of these sparrows' wintering areas are creeping further north?

But this winter of 1970 their threatened survival caused us no small concern during the incessant storms, the deep snow, and Arctic weather.

The first inkling that a winged predator had found easy hunting amid the large number of birds congregating noisily around the feeding place came on Christmas Eve. Tell-tale impressions appeared in the snow, each filled with a small pathetic heap of volatile feathers, blue ones in one place, yellow in another, clearly identifying the victims. That was all. No tracks led away from the imprints. The predator was a barred owl.

The barred owl is not a conspicuous bird-eater. According to a study of the diets of hawks and owls in Ontario, only

14.8% of this owl's food was found to be birds. The rest was made up principally of shrews and rodents. In our forests the barred owl hunts mice, varying hares, red squirrels and flying squirrels. And thereby hangs this tale.

It happened that two pine martens, one with a small mark on its left flank, had during the past two winters included our premises within their rather extensive hunting areas. In prime fur these lithe, middle-sized weasels are charming creatures – alert, intense, mercurial, of a soft warm brown colour lightly shifting into warm beige on the throat and where the long guard hairs part or shorten from wear. Their eyes gleam like black beads under pointed ears in the triangular face; the small wet nose, keenly sensitized to every scent, twitches. Nothing escapes their awareness. For their size they climb almost as smartly as the squirrels. They run with their long bodies undulating, two feet planted, one slightly ahead of the other, to form the characteristic paired weasel tracks. The martens also hunt mice, shrews, snowshoe hares, and sometimes grouse, but their staple support is the red squirrel.

For decades the ubiquitous red squirrels had lived in uncontrolled proliferation at Pimisi Bay and served themselves well from the bottomless munificence of our feeders. Now at last they found their match in the martens. The squirrels disappeared. Or, more truthfully, they made themselves scarce, spreading out into their respective territories, and moving with great caution.

To what degree of efficiency the martens actually controlled the numbers of red squirrels, I found hard to assess. I speculated upon their hunting techniques. A squirrel is much quicker, a much more agile climber than the marten, and intensely alert to events in its surroundings. Innumerable times I saw a marten and a squirrel separated only by a few dozen feet. But the marten made no attempt to chase it, no effort to threaten its safety.

In winter when the snow is deep the red squirrel's tunnelled traffic lanes offer it innumerable and handy escapeways. It need never be caught. The flying squirrel, even more nimble, quicker than its red cousin, is not earth-bound. Cornered aloft, it can easily disengage itself from hot pursuit simply by

floating into the air on its wings of extended skin. To antici-
pate the downfall and be there in time to catch the flying
squirrel is hardly within the capacities of most predators.
Indeed, the predator's chances of success are small and
elusive. The balance of opportunity between the hunter's
successful catch and the prey's lucky escape is set very fine.
No predator comes by its dinner too easily. An accidental
encounter, a blocked escape route, a sneaking surprise visit at
a red squirrel's winter nest or at the flying squirrel's sleeping
cavity at an inopportune moment – occasions like these may
furnish the predator its marginal chance of survival when the
snow lies soft and yard-deep on the ground.

When the storms came in February, the drifts piled up from
one minute to the other and buried the feeding places. To keep
them clear and accessible was essential for the survival of some
250 birds that were now dependent upon this supplementary
supply of winter food. We swept and shovelled away the snow.

I believe that the five sparrows represented unusually fit
and sturdy individuals. How they survived night after night of
severe cold, tucked away on their nightly roosts in a small
thick evergreen, I shall never know. They, less than any,
showed signs of strain. The large flat tray under the porch,
strewn with cracked corn on top of dry sand, appeared to be
their life-saver. Forever chipper and alert, they avoided competition with blue jays and grosbeaks by coming to feed early
before these others arrived, and later at night when only the
chickadees were there, busily stoking their metabolic fires for
the coming cold night. For all of the birds it held true,
however, that the colder the night, the later they left their
roosts, and the shorter was their day because they went to
roost earlier. The extension of the long night and fast seemed
an anomaly. But in an important study on the black-capped
chickadee in Alaska* in winter, it was shown that the shortened time of activity during very cold days was linked to an
increased intensity of feeding, indicating an interesting way of
conserving energy.

Only the weaklings succumbed. An evening grosbeak,
hunched and shivering, was buffeted by the throngs of

---

*Kessel, Wilson Bulletin 88, p. 59.

energetic competitors as it fed ravenously. Suddenly it fell asleep, beak tucked into fluffy scapulars, and then it awoke and fed again. That night it came to the sunflower-seed feeder suspended under the eave by my window. It fell asleep on the rim; there was nothing to tell it was alive except the light shiver of fluffed feathers as it drew breath. The full moon rose upon the coldest night of the winter. I would see a bird die, die in its sleep on the roost, the easiest, most imperceptible way to die for any living creature. No struggle, no fight, merely a cessation.

But through that long cold night I saw not death but the flicker of life miraculously keeping the sleeping body of a bird stubbornly alive. When light came it was still asleep. Through the cold mists the sun rose, round and red. As it came out above the jagged tree-top silhouettes that edged the horizon, the grosbeak suddenly awoke and darted away.

When the weather worsened, the barred owl came closer to the feeding-station. Only after it was all over did I realize the full extent of its struggle for existence. There were few snowshoe hares in the region; their population cycle happened to be at its lowest level. The ruffed grouse profited by the deep snow in safe escape and shelter. The two martens and a red fox were strong competitors for the prey that was available. Their tastes ran parallel to the owl's. The snow, trackless above but tunnelled deep below the surface, kept the small mammals in safety, out of sight. Near the feeders the owl took another evening grosbeak, and yet another bird. This time it was a small one, a chickadee.

As the storms raged and piled up the snow-drifts, the owl began to slow down perceptibly. It slept a great deal, perched high in the naked top of a dead pine, motionless. Angered at the sight of it, the blue jays mobbed it, dashed at it, screaming raucously. The owl sat with its eyes closed, unperturbed. Without warning, it softly floated to the ground. Slowly it crawled under the protecting branches of a small spruce tree.

We found it there warm, light as a feather, emaciated under its thick aerated barred and spotted plumage. And only as we carried it away did the blue jays cease their mobbing.

Part Five

The Natural Response

April 12, and dusk was about to fall after a fine, sunny, early spring day. The snow was melting rapidly, although stubborn drifts still lingered where the sun could not reach them in the hidden hollows of the forest. Back a piece, beyond the brow of the hill the ruffed grouse had drummed in the morning for the first time.

He came down the hill on to the back lawn. He seemed to float. His banded fan of a tail fully opened tilted slowly from side to side in proud rhythmic display. His wings trailed – stiffly – the tips almost touching the ground. The magnificent silky night-black ruff, fully erected and trembling, circled his small cockerel-like head. He ran forward with a few mincing steps. He shook the ruff, stopped. He pecked at the ground hastily, emphatically, picked nothing, an act of pretense, without reality. Again he ran forward, his steps so quick, so short, that he seemed to float. He stopped, shook the ruff, a gesture full of show, his small head embedded within a circle of shiny silky black fluff. Again and again he repeated this series of highly dramatic attitudes and movements as he proceeded on to a ramp of residual snow.

There was the female, the object of the cock's elaborate approach. She was walking leisurely about, picking tidbits from the ground. Did she not see him? The cock's display became more intense, more heated as the distance between them narrowed. He ran up to her. . . with a whirr of wings she suddenly took off and landed far above him on the branch of a young balsam fir. Abruptly stopped in his tracks, the cock stood motionless, holding the pose, holding her with his eyes. For 10 minutes he stood there, eyes fixed on the hen on the branch, a frozen statue. Finally the hen moved, slowly, carefully tracing her steps along the branch. She crouched and then glided down to a landing some distance away. The cock rushed in pursuit still in full display.

Three times the cock repeated the complete sequence of his courtship rituals with the interplay of responses between the pair the same, movement for movement. But today was not her day. The lack of encouragement weighed upon him. And at long last the cock gave up, folded together his tail, smoothed his trembling ruff and disappeared behind a snow-drift. The scene had endured before our fascinated eyes exactly 56 minutes.

Through the ages the ruffed grouse's courtship ceremonies have developed to facilitate the approach of the cock to the hen in the sexual and reproductive game of a species promiscuous in habits. There is no attachment on the part of either male or female; it is a liaison of full freedom. So the various parts of the ceremony are full of drama, purpose and symbolism, the languid tilting of the spread tail, the aggressively dropped wings, the exaggerations involved in the mincing steps and the shaking of the ruff; all these enhance the cock's image of impressive outline and sexual seductiveness. And the pretence pecking movements referring to feeding still further enforce the persuasive powers of the desirable male.

When the time is ripe and the weather is warmer, this loose relationship introduced with the drumming and the elaborate displays reaches its climax during the last weeks of May. Later, in a hollow between two roots of an evergreen lined with dead leaves, the hen deposits a dozen or so pale buff fertilized eggs. With all the excitement drained from her blood, she patiently sits on them and warms them. They hatch about 24 days later. It takes some time for all the chicks to break out of the shells into the living world. But no sooner is the last chick dry before mother and progeny, in a softly clucking and piping flock, abandon the nest to vanish into the greater safety of summer's rich ground cover.

Self-preservation is in all living creatures an elementary and a dominant urge. An instinctive aversion to the too-close proximity of another is part of it. Among birds, it is a pronounced phenomenon. In their relationships within their own species as well as with other species and animals, it plays an important role. Witness their volatility, their state of being constantly on the *qui vive*. The reserved zone, also called individual distance, beyond which approach is not tolerated varies in size from species to individuals, and from almost touching distance to yards. The accessibility of a bird changes also with the seasons, with the cycles of reproduction, with various activities, such as feeding and resting, as well as with its moods. Actual fighting is sometimes spawned by transgression at inopportune movements across the line. But the extent to which confrontations are either successfully avoided or eliminated is remarkable. In the scheme of nature confrontations are uneconomical and hence counteracted. The checks are numerous. The interplay between an animal's natural responses to the exigencies of situations and circumstances, and their impact upon companions, enemies and the environment is, in fact, the balance of nature in action.

Jays of a Northern Forest

Like the whisperings of the forest the grey jay moves. Its flight is like a soft sigh, deftly evasive amid the conifers, the bird insisting not upon attention and glamour. The jay perches in a tree-top, surveys the land, calls. Its voice is loud – then it fades and grows silent. The jay is gone.

They used to be called Canada jays. Their Latin name, *Perisoreus canadensis*, suggests that they live only in Canada, but this is not strictly true. They are known by many names: meat bird, moose bird, whiskey-jack. The last comes from an Indian word by which the natives of North America knew them long before the white man ever saw them. Now they are called grey jays and this is a good and true name.

The grey jays live in the vast forests across the continent. In these wild regions many bogs and swamps give rich growth to evergreens of all kinds. Tamarack and thick young spruces thrive here and the last kind seems to have a special attraction for the grey jays. But they also like dry forests where brown leaves lie curled beneath the deciduous trees, where sunlight sifts through the branches upon leaf-mold and mosses. Here they may even nest, provided the well-feathered evergreens are not missing.

At Pimisi Bay, the grey jays appear irregularly at any time of the year. About once in every three years, sometimes less often, some of them spend most of the fall, winter, and spring in this neighbourhood.

Out of the half-light of the forest the grey jays emerge soundlessly. The uneven edges of the pinions of their wings and tails give them a ragged look. Only when caught in good light do they display their true beauty. Then the exquisite shadings of their plumage, from the lightest grey to almost black, become visible, sometimes with a bluish tint on the back and shoulders, like shadows on snow on sunlit winter days. As if pushed back over their crowns, a dark cap frames a light grey frontal spot, round as a penny. Their cinnamon-brown eyes look large, almost thrush-like, and shine with an oddly knowing expression.

The silent appearance of the grey jays imbues the chickadees and the nuthatches with fright. The short-necked long-tailed shadow that the jay casts upon the ground causes them to "freeze" motionless, or flee shrieking into the nearest cover. But as the jays continue to come and go with no movement, nor even a predatory look in their soft brown eyes, to bear out the fears of the small birds, their frightened reaction to the hawk-like shapes soon wears away.

The movements of the grey jays have a peculiarly bouncing quality, as if the laws of gravity were relaxed in their case. This is partly true. They are as large in size as the blue jays – their official length measurement is practically the same – but in weight the greys are about one-third lighter than the blues. Their voluminous contour is deceiving. Their plumage consists of exceptionally long and silky feathers, especially on the breast and belly, that keep the birds beautifully warm in the severe climate to which they belong.

Many are the tales from the woodsmen's camps in the far

northern forests about the tameness of the grey jays. They sometimes act with a boldness that few other birds display and some of them are more unafraid and enterprising than others. On a first visit to our feeding-station they never seem to be bothered by that feeling of insecurity in a strange place that most other birds show. Nor do they hesitate to approach the feeders at once, as if they knew already of the good food to be found there, without first having to watch how the other birds feed from them. To connect man with food comes naturally to them. Nearly always, whenever they come across hunters, trappers, and loggers in the bush, they find meat, blood, and offal in their tracks. Scavengers, like the raven and the crow, they look inquisitively for their share in the bounty on which they often depend in winter.

It is against the essence of the wild bird to be tame. With the jays, a strong urge to eat is mixed with innocence and makes them seem fearless; however, as they continue to visit our feeders their brave front vanishes with the loss of their great hunger, and they become shyer instead of bolder.

The occasions of the grey jays' prolonged fall-to-spring stops at Pimisi Bay always coincided with years in which they were also on the move in other parts of the land. These years were notable, too, for a scarcity of coniferous seeds and berries. Birds of the more northern latitudes often find their larders empty, because they depend largely on foods such as the seeds of trees, which fluctuate in abundance from year to year. The increasing difficulty of finding sufficient food drives them to move out of these areas in search of better living conditions.

The long-established feeding place at Pimisi Bay had the opposite effect upon the jays which found it in the course of their wanderings. They stopped. They fed eagerly on the suet, kitchen scraps, and lard-pudding, our own special concoction. The supply was inexhaustible. They lingered – they stayed all winter and into the late spring. I trapped and banded all of them, including coloured bands so as to recognize them individually. Strange as it seems, for birds that are supposed to be a "resident" species, not one grey jay stayed longer than to the end of the nesting season. Nor did any of them return.

Blue jays come back year after year, sometimes to stay over the winter, sometimes to go on farther south and return to their nesting grounds in the spring. The banded grey jays vanished from our forest; every grey jay (except one) that came was a stranger, an unmarked bird. Later, as will be shown, there were exceptions.

Mated grey jays live together throughout the year and probably do not part until death takes one of them. The bond between them is strong. Where one is, the other is not far away. Often you may find them sitting together in some secluded spot and if you are not too far away you may hear them exchanging their secret parrot-like communications in hushed voices.

With birds that live together in this manner all the time, courtship is often a protracted game that may last for months. The short-lived intensive courtship is only for those that must cram this important part of their reproductive life into a few days or weeks, like many migrants do. When the grey jays arrive at Pimisi Bay in the fall, it is by no means too early to find them side by side, billing in their own peculiar way, opening their bills at each other or touching each other's mandibles. In moments of heightened excitement they engage in a kind of courtship feeding, but without any food passing between them. This "token feeding" continues throughout the nesting season. Only rarely do the grey jays complete the act and offer or accept food between them, like the blue jays often do during their pre-nesting period. Sometimes one of the grey jays puts its bill into the nape feathers of its partner and ruffles them gently. In a pose of mild ecstasy and giving mewing notes, the mate accepts the caress with obvious pleasure. Those who have read Dr. Konrad Lorenz' book, *King Solomon's Ring*, will remember the same behaviour described in jackdaws, but with the difference that the attractive nape spot in them is light grey, and almost black in the light-coloured jays.

In many birds with more or less strongly developed no-madic impulses, faithfulness to the special breeding territory is not always a common trait. The existence of abundant food in one place and not in the other influences their movements more than the homing tendency does. Plenty of food is also required for the task of raising the young broods. With our grey jays, nestings always followed their long winter visits at Pimisi Bay. Their breeding season began in March when the melting snows gradually uncovered the ground and the sun took the frost out of the upper layers of the forest debris.

The jays built one nest within sight of our house and tucked it into the upright crotch of a young spruce. They got no further than laying a few eggs in it when a porcupine decided to climb the tree. The eggs were still intact after the porcupine was persuaded to come down again, but the sight of this awful threat was too much for the jays. They deserted the nest and were never seen again.

Another pair of jays settled high on the embankment of an elongated lake whose outlet formed a crooked chute. The distant roar of this falling water filled the air. In a spot with a wide view over the wilderness stretching beyond the lake to the horizon, they had securely attached their nest close to the trunk of a bushy young spruce. Their massive structure was made of stout twigs on the outside, with a bowl of grasses, dead leaves, and cocoon fabric, inside. In this way the jays achieved a remarkable creation of warmth and insulation against freezing weather for the five eggs that lay, beautifully white and spotted with olive-brown, with their small ends neatly turned inwards upon a soft bed of hairs and feathers.

The owners of this nest returned from a short foraging trip. Uttering mellow notes, they stepped around the nest and over it, apparently undecided which one of them ought to sit down on it. They stretched their necks and opened their bills but no food passed from one to the other. In growing excitement both crouched and shivered their wings until finally one of them entered the nest and sat down on the eggs, carefully adjusting them under its broodspot. The other followed and sat down on top of the first bird, their bodies slightly cross-wise. The one covering the eggs, with only its head and tail showing, was embedded deeply under the long fluffed feathers of the one on top.

I watched this nest for five whole days. The two jays incubated together, sometimes for several hours on end. Their periods of rest and feeding were short and they seldom left the nest unattended except when disturbed. They shifted about in sitting on top of each other while on the nest, but one of them spent more time in direct contact with the eggs than the other and she showed this by having a larger broodspot. Furthermore, she was the one that laid the eggs. Everytime the birds met, whether at the nest or elsewhere, they repeated their prolonged ritual of stepping around each other, billing, and exchanging notes. Theirs was a close relationship.

An egg broke in the nest. The jays ate the eggshell and drank the liquid that spilled from the evidently infertile egg. By this time they had been sitting on their eggs for at least 21 days, four days longer than the incubation period of grey jays normally lasts.

Two days later three of the remaining eggs had disappeared but the fourth, also infertile, was reposing in the nest still warm. At a short distance the two jays sat in a young spruce side by side, whispering soft notes. They would not return to the nest. They gave no sign of even remembering it. They lifted and flew in circles among the trees. They rose into the air, but soon came down again on set wings, weaving in and out of the evergreens, occasionally striking a branch with a snapping noise. Their enchanted spot still held them as if by a resilient thread that would not break. Once again they flew high above the tallest pine, halted as if held there on a strong wind, then slid into a wide loop across the lake out of sight northwards into the wilderness, never to return.

Fourteen years later, a lone grey jay arrived at our feeding station in early October. Judged by its measurements and behaviour, this bird was a male and he got the name M-1. A day or two later, a pair arrived – M-2, and his mate, F-1.

No brotherly love was lost between M-1 and M-2. In bouncing passes they chased each other from one end of the premises to the other. F-1's behaviour did not improve matters. She chased nobody, but she presented herself to both rivals in submissive attitudes – she crouched, and she shivered her wings, with her head lifted, her bill wide open. This, naturally, only increased the belligerency between the two males. They intensified their pursuits and punctuated them with loud utterances. Once M-2 bore M-1 to the ground in the hottest combat I ever witnessed between grey jays. M-1 escaped with a piercing outcry as if he were badly hurt, but he was not.

During the first part of their stay in the neighbourhood, the three jays roosted in the evergreens overshadowing our house. They awakened early but did not leave their roosts at once. Through the stillness of dawn, jay called to jay with three or four loud ringing notes, one jay answering the other and sending forth the call to the third.

Perhaps in this case the situation carried with it a special incentive for the ardent trio to express themselves vocally. They uttered a surprising variety of sounds, some gruff and raucous, some shrill, some full-toned and often purely musical. The harshest one, with an overtone of aggressiveness, was the scolding note which sounded like a short burst of toneless laughter. The softest was the alarm note, reminding me of a monosyllabic toned-down owl hoot, repeated twice. The most amazing was the canary-like whisper song given in moments of frustration, when the jays wanted to do something that the situation did not permit.

F-2's appearance put an end to most of this after she paired with M-1. The hostilities between the males decreased partly because good reason for fighting no longer existed, since each of them now had a mate, and partly because the jays no longer lived near the feeding place, which they had claimed simultaneously for their own private property. Instead, both pairs withdrew to other premises in different directions, whence they paid their visits to the feeders much less often and usually at staggered times. Battles flared up anew only when one of the males trespassed upon the space around a female which was mated to the other. Then swift chases ensued.

Exciting developments appeared to be pending when a third female appeared. I knew she was a new-comer because she wore no band on her leg. Nothing happened. There were no fights. Within less than a week I understood that the female, F-3, had joined M-1 and his mate F-2 and was obviously accepted by them with what seemed to be bosom friendship. All three came to the feeding-station together, and fed together, and they went away together, back along their selected routes to their own home area.

A month later a similar trilateral relationship developed with the arrival of three new jays, suggesting that associations of this kind may be no more exceptional among grey jays than they are among many other species of birds. They depend on circumstances, such as the feeding place luring them together within a limited area, with the females in the majority, and unmated. This, at least, was true with our grey jays.

The strange case from 14 years before, never explained, of the two jays trying in vain to bring life into the five eggs in the nest, comes to mind. And, because the female grey jay normally incubates the eggs alone, without help from her mate, could these two actually have been the surviving females of such a friendly triumvirate, doing exactly what they were meant to do?

The crow family, to which the jays also belong, has long been considered one of the most intelligent among birds. To this I subscribe.

Of two grey jays, one was very shy and the other bold. With the blue jays around, the greys must be hand-fed. The blue ones are aggressive and quickly snap up the food thrown out without giving anyone else a chance, while the greys just sit and watch the food disappear. The bolder one needs no lesson to take food from my hand; the shy one has great difficulty in overcoming its timidity.

So today, on a cold and snowy spring morning, I take pity on the shy one, dispense with the lesson and throw out a piece of lard pudding, the jays' favourite delicacy. The piece falls on the other side of a three-foot high wire fence. But instead of frantically trying to get at the tidbit through the wire as every other bird would, the shy one without hesitation flies over the top of the fence and secures the piece. The morsel is turned over and over in the bird's mouth until it takes the shape of an oval lump heavily coated with saliva. This the bird deposits, well preserved and safe, into a suitable cranny in the bushy spruce, for the greys, like the blue jays, are great hoarders.

By late May the grey jays' brood is out of the nest. Together with their parents, they tour the feeding place. One of the parents hops around collecting a load of pudding. But at the sight of another tempting piece, instead of dropping the load and forgetting it to pick up the new piece as the blue jays do, this bird lays the load down carefully, swallows the new piece, *then picks up the load again* and carries it to the next glob of tempting food. Surprising behaviour – I test it. Again and again the bird repeats the procedure and, finally, flies away with its crop and mouth filled to capacity.

Whether these two examples of behaviour would pass scientific scrutiny as spontaneous adaptive acts, I cannot guarantee. Nevertheless, these grey jays showed more than the usual amount of grasp than their counterparts have been known to display.

My Conditioned Chickadees

From the beginning it was never my intention to tame the black-capped chickadees that came to our feeding-station. In my opinion, taming spoils the true character of the wild creature. But when, about 40 years ago, one of the chickadees showed an unusual disregard for my nearness, and indicated a willingness, without a great deal of persuasion, to come to my hand, I decided that this association would be wholly the responsibility of the chickadees.

I never regretted this decision. What the chickadees have since shown me of their elfin character; what they have taught me of their reactions; all was done in an atmosphere of liberty. There was only the seed – the magic sunflower seed. The seed pulled away the fear that at first separated them from me. It spanned the bridge of harmonious relationships between us and established the only kind of foundation, I would say, upon which a true appreciation of nature's creatures is built. Whatever compulsion that the seed may have exerted at the start in forging the bond, vanished later, and was of no account.

As I said, there was at first one particular chickadee. This one I called Peet, by reason of a special little note he gave as he approached me. Most of the other chickadees also gave this note in the way of an "alert," which had the effect of catching the attention of the other birds as well as of me. But the second Peet, that came into existence a good many years later, was not given his name for the same reason. He got his because he, of all the chickadees of my closer acquaintance, most resembled the first Peet in character and consequently influenced events in the same way. Both lived in the forest around our house; and being at home is very important in directing the behaviour of birds in particular, and also of other creatures. Both chickadees possessed that innate quality of enterprise that creates pioneers and which, in effect, was the root and origin of the good understanding that came to exist, at times, between the birds and me.

This is how it came about.

Our chickadees had never in their lives, as far as I know, seen a sunflower seed. The first time I put a few of them on their dinner plate, most of the birds did not recognize the seeds for anything except something strange. But Peet, and that was the first time I distinguished him, pecked at the seed. He took it and turned it around in his bill. This was important. In some way it imparted to him the condition of the kernel. Was it a good seed, a thick seed, a light seed, a poor seed? Whether he could hear it move inside the shell as he shifted it about, or somehow judged its weight, I never knew. But he and the other chickadees nearly always discarded a bad seed, and sometimes, also, a good one.

Having made the test, he flew to a tree. There he put the seed under both of his feet and held it fast against the branch. This is the way all chickadees and, I believe, all titmice handle a seed. And because they *know* this, without needing to learn it, it is an instinctive act. He split the seed open by hammering elfin blows upon it with his bill. When he did not succeed in opening it the first time, he turned it around and tried another spot. It cracked, and he pulled open the shell, letting the fragments fall to the ground.

Peet usually ate the kernel, but sometimes he stored it. This happened in times when there was much food available and comparatively few chickadees to share it or, to put it in other words, when the food supply was a little heavy in the environmental balance. Nearly always, autumn was the best time to store things away. But there were other times, too, except in the breeding season, when the chickadees stored their surplus rations.

With great care Peet selected his storing place in the wedge between two twigs, or in a curled piece of bark, or in any convenient fissure where it could be securely tucked in. Often after having deposited the seed, he pulled it out again, flew off with it, searched for another place, found it, and pushed in the seed. *There!* At some time during the countless inspections he performed later of every twig of every tree in his quest for food, he or somebody else found that kernel and ate it.

This gave me to understand that the sunflower seed had rapidly won high favour with him. With increasing assurance, Peet repeated the act again, and then again.

The other chickadees looked on. I knew that they were curious and afraid, interested, and hungry. I knew because some of them lifted the feathers of their black caps, and smoothed them down again. Others opened their bills without uttering a sound, and still others made chewing motions with their bills and tongue. This chewing had really nothing to do with their eating, or wanting to eat, because they did it, not from anticipation, but from not being able to eat at that particular moment when their timidity overruled their hunger. A few more courageous chickadees became so incited by the sight of Peet plucking so much good food from my hand, that they made dare-devil flights to half-way between their perch and me, then head-over-tails flew back to the perch, often with cries of real or mock fright. Each such attempt brought them a little closer to their goal – the seed – until finally they snatched it and flew off with it at great speed.

This was the way that the two Peets became the "key-birds." Thus, unknowingly, they worked upon the inclinations of their chickadee followers, inducing them to repeat their own successful acts to the advantage of all concerned.

When this stage was reached, the chickadees began to learn things in connection with me and the seed. They found new and convenient ways of seizing the seed, no longer only from my open hand, but from my pockets or from my lips as they alighted blithely on my nose or eyeglasses. At times when the seed and I vanished into the house, some of them clung to the edge of the eave or an icicle and looked in. Some, like suspended marionettes, hovered at the window when they saw me inside. Some followed me from window to window, alighted on the sill, sat, looked in, then pecked at the pane, chagrined that they could not reach me. My immediate response to these charming sights and sounds was, of course, to go out and give them a seed. Gradually, they learned that these activities of theirs usually resulted in the reappearance of both me and the seeds. And from then on I had only to move away from the window to have the chickadees fly directly to the door where, sure enough, I appeared and they got their due reward.

By this time the chickadees began to connect me with the seed so closely that the seed and I became, in their eyes, one object. This led me to wonder how exactly did they know me? What in my appearance made them distinguish me with such consistency, that they came volplaning down to me from 60-foot tree-tops the instant they glimpsed me, that they flew under roofs and inside of houses to find me, and even into my car before I left or at my return from a trip? All of them were by no means so adept at recognizing me. But there were Peet and half a dozen of his followers whose capacities in this respect seemed to have few limits.

In order to find out more about this interesting behaviour, I travelled in a boat out on the nearby lake at various distances from the shore. Chickadees are reluctant to cross open spaces, even on land, and they do so willingly only in places they are used to flying across, or those which they cross in a flock. Even then, a faint-hearted one, when only half-way across, may turn back, or drop down into shrub or tree cover. In spite of this, Peet came to me over the open water, a distance between 150 and 200 feet. Intrepidly, he launched himself upon these flights, sometimes in a good wind that blew his tail sideways, a sweet and touching little figure, alone in mid-air. When he arrived finally at my boat, he pitched on my head or came to the tip of my finger. Having received his seed from me, he made the return trip flying low and direct to the safety of the lake shore. Most of the other chickadees never came any farther away from shore than 25 to 50 feet, becoming prey to all kinds of distractions, such as chasing a companion or pecking at some food. Only a few matched Peet's flights over the water. But beyond these distances from shore, I might as well have been invisible; they appeared not to see me, although with a bird's sharp eyesight, it is unlikely that they could *not* detect me.

One day I lay down for a nap on the floor under the roof of the porch – a warm and sunny place. If I thought that I would be well hidden from the chickadees, I was quickly put to shame. Peet came, perched in my hair, looked for a seed in my hand, and found it. After Peet, several others came and did the same. My noon-hour sleep was ruined, but I really did not mind. It was an interesting discovery to find that the chickadees recognized me, even when I was lying down, and not in my usual upright posture.

After this I did everything I could to keep the chickadees from distinguishing the outlines of my person. I crouched, and I covered myself over, to see what would happen. The chickadees were not deceived. They had always seen, or did see, enough of me to shatter my most painstaking efforts to hide from them. Then I remembered how song-birds see and recognize hawks and owls, whether these predators are in flight or perching. I could only conclude that the chickadees recognized me in the very same way, no matter what I wore, or whether I was upright, or lying down. The picture the chickadees had of me was that of a whole figure, much simplified perhaps, if we could draw it exactly as they saw it, but nevertheless a highly adequate and appropriate picture.

I was never able to feel that the chickadees really knew me personally. Any man that came up our path to the house was to them also a seed container. When I stood beside the stranger,

the birds *preferred* to come to me, but only until my companion offered them a seed. After that, their preference for me
quickly vanished. Many birds are able to distinguish one
person from another, as we have learned from the fascinating
accounts of Dr. Konrad Lorenz, and other specialists in the
study of animal behaviour. The difference between the en-
vironments in the learning of the wild birds of these experi-
menters and of mine may be this – that these people lived in
heavily populated communities where it was necessary for the
birds to learn to distinguish one person who fed them from a
multitude of indifferent ones. I live in the wilderness. There
are not enough people here to make it rewarding for the
chickadees to tell us apart.

At the time when I knew the first Peet, I owned a blond
muskrat coat with a dark collar. The first time I appeared
among the chickadees wearing this coat, the effect on them
was spectacular. They flew away with every sign of distress.
They refused to come near me. They went into a "mobbing"
scene, as they often do at the sight of a dangerous predator,
with loud scolding, wing-flicking, short flights from twig to
twig, and chasing of each other, which they did simply
because they were too excited to contain themselves. Their
noise and excited movements attracted every other bird in the
vicinity.

Plainly they took me for a fur-bearing animal of the kind
they were used to seeing – a short-tailed weasel, a mink, or
possibly a muskrat. But the image was grossly exaggerated.
And this led to the release of a behaviour pattern matching the
intensity of the nervous tension caused by the sight. Thus I
was and I remained unacceptable whenever I wore the coat.

The Eternal Alliance

For a very long time I have known the eastern phoebe. This enchanting grey-frocked bird, with its sharp black eyes and an elegantly teetering tail that looks as if it were hooked on a swivel. It is a common bird, familiar to most bird-watchers.

In the course of the years, without posing any threat to the birds' independence and wildness, a closeness developed in our relationship, an alliance, I might say, the kind of natural, desirable and useful one between living creatures that affords opportunities to advance certain expedients important to each.

Artful and resourceful, the phoebe is a nest-builder of note. And a great deal of interest is to be gleaned from this brief interval in the bird's life, from the interplay between the partners of a pair and the impact of circumstances upon their activities, things not too readily revealed except through prolonged acquaintance.

Fifty years ago the area around Pimisi Bay on the threshold of the great boreal forests of the north was almost empty of people. The phoebe lived here, returning each spring to the same place where it had spent last summer's nesting season. When the ice lay still soggy on the lake and drifts of snow lingered deep in the dark wet shadows of the rocky ground, the phoebe was the first of the entirely insect-eating birds to appear. Already the sun had brought out hordes of flying insects, gnats, small flies, spiders, butterflies, even an odd mosquito looking lonesome and bewildered in its premature emergence. Bare spots on the ground fairly crawled with reanimated insectlife when the strong beams of direct sunshine fell upon them. Provided the sun shone, there usually was enough to eat. But to arrive ahead of the weather was hazardous and adventurous male phoebes required a special aptitude to find and to catch insects retired from the chilling winds and depressed by the creeping shadows.

For a day or a night, maybe longer, the bird early returned may well tolerate, without impairment, a reduced diet. Under the skin, in the hollows of its bone structure and muscles, sometimes small deposits of fat remain – from earlier migration reserves – to tide it over. But should the north winds persist, as they often do on this 46th parallel in the spring, leaving the bird scant opportunity to restock, then the hunger emergency quickly arises, often fatally.

When we settled here, the phoebes were well established around a sandy bank where they found attractive nest sites in tiny caves under the overhanging turf and interlaced roots. Often tradition guides not only the migrating bird or pair, but also their successors, back to the same favoured place where phoebes nested before so long as it holds the specific features they need for successful breeding.

In this bank habitat, presently, local changes occurred. Erosion altered the topography of the bank, eliminating the overhang. Also the cyclic development of natural things brought a sudden increase in predators, making the locality insecure. This drove the phoebes to seek more suitable environs.

They found it not far away, around our newly built buildings. Here was to be found the full set of the phoebe's nesting requirements: shelving to hold the nest on ledges above windows and doors, walls and nooks which provided background security for the sitting female, and under the overhanging eaves, shelter from the weather. And so, ever since the first female abandoned the bank territory 41 years ago, one or two pairs of phoebes have maintained uninterrupted traditional territorial arrangements around our buildings.

The move was fine. Yet the first change-over from a place to which the male in particular harboured so strong a territorial attachment was not that easy. He hesitated, flew back and forth from the garage to the bank. For all the dominance the female exercises in the phoebes' family affairs, the male is prey to certain sensibilities that make any drastic change of the environment a wrench for him. For he is the one that establishes the territory before the female arrives. He is content not only to make himself known there by his singing and to fight intrusions by strangers of his own kind; he also looks for, finds and visits – sometimes sits on – potential nest sites. And this is important. Yet, as meaningful as these delectable volant inspections of his may be in presenting her with a number of previewed choices when she arrives, they represent all of real practical value that he contributes to the creation of the nest. As will be seen, a residual sense for the nest remains with him throughout none the less, and occasionally influences his behaviour.

The female's arrival caused the male to virtually stop singing. She was there, and the advertising portion of his vocal activities had lost part of its purpose. With the male in close attendance, the female lost no time in looking over potential nest sites. Together they flew up to every promising shelf. She sat on each one. He, too, sat on it; or he merely perched on the edge, flipping his tail. The female pressed her breast down and made molding motions; she shook, feeling out the form of the place. She lingered. They flew out together and came back, fluttering softly, intimately, their tails whipping up and down and around. Watching them, one is impressed with the togetherness of the pair, with the symbolism of their movements.

How long a time they spent on this business largely depended on the weather. Warm breezes hastened proceedings; cool blustery conditions created a great urgency to find enough food, leaving little time for other activities. The female was tempted to carry the first tuft of green moss, the first pellet of mud, to the site. And then, for several days, a week maybe, she did not show the slightest interest in it. But returning sunshine, a flow of warm southerly air, lifted the pressures of food finding. And she went back to work on the structure with great industry, sometimes from morning until dusk, for four, five, eight or nine days.

Closely interlaced with these preliminary nest-building activities was the unfolding of their courtship. Could any better stimulus be devised than these visits together to various likely nesting places, fostering the mutual tolerance that leads to mating between two birds of the same species, sharing that one piece of land? They fly about together, their movements excite, their soft notes communicate, their contact impassions. Dusk begins to fall after a long day. Suddenly for a brief moment the male regains the leading role. Lightning-like, with a scream, he pursues her, pounces upon her and brings her to the ground. It is an act full of force and exuberance. He repeated it once – a second time – three times.

Wings aflutter, she rises from the impact, smooth, beautiful – and he lets her go. She flies to the window ledge and the collection of mud and moss she has been working with all day. And there, alighting on the edge of it, she settles to roost alone.

In this way, without much ado, the phoebes took possession of our man-made structures and there selected the spots best suited for their needs. They moved like shadows, inconspicuously vanishing, reappearing. And often, before the eggs were laid, I did not know if they were still there.

The building of the phoebes' nest was an intriguing operation, full of variations. We put up shelves to assist them. More often than not they ignored the shelves and nested in narrower and darker corners, where the bird hardly had room enough to turn around. We took the hint and moved some of the shelves to similar places, and in time some of these were preferentially accepted.

With each start of the nest-building the male turns into the follower, while the female reserves the big job for herself. Now the dominant figure of the pair, she becomes engrossed in the task. Faithfully, the male escorts her to and from the places where she collects her materials and then watches her work from a distance. On a rare occasion after she leaves he may alight on the nest, sit, and perhaps gingerly let his breast nudge the stuff, making half a turn molding it, only to dash quickly away.

Meanwhile, the female finds and carries tiny billfuls of soft green moss alternately with equally tiny billfuls of mud. Far back on the shelf she puts the stuff. Mud and clay are plastered onto the support and into the mass of green moss. Right from the start, like a sculptress, she fashions the nest-cup. Gradually the walls of the cup rise around her until they reach the height and width required. Her main tool is her breast. Pressing it down into the materials, she turns first one way, then in reverse. With wings spread, tail teetering to maintain balance, she scratches vigorously with her feet to push the breast deeper into the stuff, and it leaves there the exact impression of her body. Now she is off to fetch another billful of green moss, another gob of mud. Vibrating mightily, she sticks the new load deep into the mass. Not a single piece of moss nor a gob of mud is added without these dainty trembling motions. Often she tries so hard to make the loads stick that they shake off. And then, all finished, with an elegant swoop she is over the edge, uttering soft notes as if the nest were a thing alive. Quickly the male flies out to meet her. But she shoots past him to fetch another billful of moss or a pellet of mud. By the time she starts carrying dead grasses, frizzly dry weeds, hairs and other fuzz gathered where I shake the rugs, the nest is a solid mass around three inches high of already slightly faded green moss.

The phoebes' predilection, already mentioned, for "natural" places in which to build their nests, as opposed to our roomy shelves, has led to interesting discoveries. Some of these "natural" shelves were so narrow as to necessitate the construction of some kind of additional supports. Possibly due to the air being of exactly the right dryness on occasion, or the clay being of the right kind, quick to dry, some of these females met with astonishing success.

One intrepid bird steadfastly refused to accept the shelf nailed above the door of the workshop, in favour of a ledge less than one inch wide above the window. Try as I might to tempt her by transferring her own gathered materials from the ledge to the shelf, she would promptly carry it back, dropping some on the way. In the end she managed to complete a structure that looked like a swallow's nest. To provide the proper inside cup size, it bulged out over the ledge, so that over half of it rested on a bracket-like support of hardened clay.

Just as the female began laying her eggs, the male vanished. Here today, gone tomorrow for him – and a hawk has eaten. It was unfortunate. But this did not deter the female from carrying out alone the full predetermined course of the nesting cycle. She sat warming the eggs for 16 days, while spring flowed into summer. On that 16th day only one crawly semblance of a bird rolled out of one single egg of her clutch of five, for there had not been time for the male to fertilize all the eggs before he vanished. Seventeen days later the youngster flew full fledged from the nest.

Another bird took a fancy to a pipe only two inches in diameter, which protruded through a wall under the eave. I thought, she'll never balance a nest on that! But the way she sat on it, the way she nudged it, fitting her breast down upon it, showed she was not going to abandon it. The moment she put the first good gob of clay on one side of it and it stuck – here was the seal of her choice. She started work that afternoon.

She used her bill like forceps, with energetic trembling action, to push and to pat moss and mud on the sides of the pipe. She brought seven loads in 30 minutes. She stood over the artwork and looked at it. Some of the mud stuck, some fell. She caught sight of a dry strand of grass, picked it up and flew away with it.

The nest shaped up like a saddle, perched on top of the pipe, moss hanging down on each side. Most of the mud dried hard and the nest was secure. Eight loads of moss and mud in one hour; 12 loads in one hour. On the eighth day the nest measured over three inches in height, beautifully hollowed to fit her body. All this time the male had been escorting her closely on her trips to and fro, watching her as she worked. Once he brought a strand of grass and laid it on the pipe, just laid it there. As dusk descended, she stopped working, flew to the nest and adjusted herself comfortably upon it.

The air was soft, full of the scent of budding leaves. Nearby a robin intoned a mellow vesper song. The male was catching flies. With his beak wide open he tumbled like a loose leaf in the wind after them, catching them as in a trap. Then he lifted and glided slowly and vibrantly upon the air, and a flight song poured from his throat, composed of trilled and whistled notes.

He sang again the next morning, this time his abrupt husky *phoe-be* songs. He sang all morning and far into the late afternoon, and he was all alone. For months afterwards the nest sat on the pipe unused, in mute evidence of the industry and adaptability of an eastern phoebe nest-builder.

There was another, and she selected a rather wide ledge running near the ceiling along the inside of the porch. She set to work on a nest, never stopping until dusk came that day. The male was not with her. Where was he? The result of her efforts was not impressive. Moss and mud were plastered along a yard-long section of the ledge. No concentration at all. What is more, she carried moss and mud, dry grasses and frilly weeds at the same time, foundation and lining materials all mixed together, and put them down with determined molding, scratching and trembling. All for nothing.

There was no nest-cup. Five days at work and no cup. No male either. Where was he? Every effort she expended came to nothing, due to the total lack of co-ordination. There was only a mess of moss and mud, dry straws and weeds.

When a male finally showed up and he began courting her, she knew how to respond, and there was no lack of co-ordination. Instinct, stereotyped behaviour patterns – call it what you will – laid down in wild things are usually so infallible that aberrations are rare. But diversity, one of nature's chief conditions for progress, constitutes, as all of us well know, together with the eternal alliance between male, female, species and environment, the warp and weft of all life.

The Red Squirrel

It was queer that Kicki should have come to me of her own accord, for it was no secret, 30 years ago, that I was unfavourably disposed towards red squirrels. She should have known this from the innumerable times that I had chased her and all her brothers and sisters, husbands and children, away from the bird feeders. Sometimes my intent had been murderous, for is there any animal around a bird-banding station as exasperating as a red squirrel? Once they have discovered that a certain place is a fine spot for good food, the little beasts are unbeatable. They will steal a run on you every time no matter what you try to do to outsmart them.

Moreover, it was difficult for me to have sympathy for an animal that had been caught, sitting on its haunches, deliberately twirling the head of a nestling junco between its paws as if it were a delectable nut. At least, this kind of behaviour *appeared* most unfortunate to one whose main interest was birds. Therefore I trapped the squirrels and carried them off without compunction to some remote woods, this being an approved way of getting rid of bothersome small mammals. Yet, no matter how many I carried away, there was always one squirrel left that would never let itself be caught. Judging from its cunning and boldness, I suspect this was Kicki, although I did not know her personally at that time.

Furthermore, my husband protested. He liked squirrels

and thought it was cruel to subject them to such abrupt changes of environment, particularly in the winter and spring. Of course, it did not suit me to agree with this, but when he began discoursing upon the evils of discrimination between races and species and upon the innate right of all creatures to live, I had to confess myself defeated. And so, from then on, the squirrels were left undisturbed.

It was not an easy time that followed. After I ceased control over them, never had these woods been so overrun by squirrels. The percentage of bird nesting failures that spring kept me under high, nervous tension. Naturally, any nest found broken up from an unknown cause, I blamed on the squirrels. As time went on I became more and more skeptical about nature's vaunted efficiency in keeping her animal populations within well-balanced proportions. Nothing whatever happened to suggest that our territory's over-taxed carrying capacity for squirrels was being levelled off, but nature works very slowly in these matters. She has lots of time, and her wheels grind into motion only after enough pressure has been maintained for a long enough period of time.

This was the way matters stood when Kicki made her first overture. In her own casual manner and in the inevitable logic of her ways, she upset most of my preconceived ideas and changed my attitude altogether toward her and her tribe. And very strange and stupid it seemed to me afterwards that I should have permitted myself to labour for so long under such misapprehensions in my dealings with Kicki and her kin. The trouble was that I had known too little about them.

At this time Kicki was nursing young. For a week previously she had appeared with her waistline near bursting. Then one bright morning she presented herself, thin as a rake and rather mangy-looking. She was shedding her winter coat, and the moult had got as far as her thighs and shoulders. Only her long thick leggings and sleeves remained therefore, and these made her look ridiculously malproportioned with her fat extremities and skinny torso.

She jerked herself down the tree-trunk close to where I sat. Obviously she associated me with a favourite food which she had observed was available after I had been seen at the special places. She was still there when I returned a little later with a box containing peanut butter. As I held it out to her she came toward me, then stopped suddenly and would come no nearer.

From then on the steps to greater intimacies were easily covered. She began to approach whenever she saw me, sniffed, twitched her tail and looked up at me with a comical inquisitive air. If I moved unexpectedly, she dashed off to a safe distance. From there she regarded me without batting an eyelid, her front paws held tight to her breast. To boost her self-assurance she scolded a little, then approached again, on trial. At long last, persuaded that I was quite agreeable to her plans, and also safe, she began to hoist herself tentatively up and up along my slacks. At the level of my hand held down at my side, she found a box of peanut butter. She settled herself comfortably to make the best of her opportunity.

After this, preliminaries were abandoned and whenever she met me she forthwith enthroned herself either on my hand or on my shoulder. When I was too busy with other things she delicately picked sunflower seeds from my lips with never a nip from her orange-coloured front teeth. Soon she boldly came in through the window to locate her tidbits. In spite of an interested cat, the inside of the building held no terror for her except for one thing. If she lost track of the way she came in, her discovery threw her into a helpless panic. While the cat looked on amazed, Kicki tore around the house like a demon, upsetting everything, until she finally found the exit that I held wide open for her.

Kicki always ate heartily. Sometimes she choked over too generous mouthfuls and then recovered by intensive swallowing. It was obvious that she expected to eat her fill at one sitting, for she was disconcerted by any interference. When she had enough she would ask for no more, turn away and make off, always by the same route, over the woodpile, up the hill, and back to her territory around the Green House.

This was her home. I never needed to linger long within this area of about two acres before I felt the tug of her claws on my clothes. Her boundaries seemed a little irregular and were, perhaps, flexible, but along one side she never went with me past a certain bubbling spring. Her nest was in a white spruce, a bulky nest that had been there for many years. Early each spring it was relined and repaired with strips of bark torn off the white cedars. With her front paws Kicki deftly rolled these strips into neat, tight balls, put them in her mouth and carried them to her spruce-top home.

On discovering her complete attachment for this piece of land, I often imagined her distress at being taken away and left to shift for herself in a strange and unknown place. How dismayed and lost she would have been, running around aimlessly, attacked and chased by the locally established squirrels, searching in vain for her well-known lanes and feeding routes! Being an old female, she might have endured added hardships before she finally resigned herself to the inevitable and found a place to settle, or possibly found her way back home. Obviously, therefore, it was cruel to move female squirrels away from their territories. As for the males, I do not know enough of their habits to guess at their reactions.

At her best, either in the summer when she was greyer, or in the winter when she was redder, Kicki was a very beautiful squirrel. She had a sleekness and a nap that set her apart. Her ears were trimmed with Mephisto tufts in winter and were quite naked in the summer. The right ear was turned over and by this one I knew her. Surrounded by a conspicuous light ring, her eyes had a deep purple lustre and were so seldom wiped with an eyelid as to appear constantly unblinking. It was odd that they reflected her emotions so little, but these were expressed by her tail, the flexible and extravagant brush that adorned her rear end. Curved tightly over her back, it declared that she was content and in a casual mood; with the tip bent outwards she was alert and on the jump; held straight behind she was decamping fast; and if it undulated sinuously, like a snake, she was in the throes of an emotional combustion, the scope and intensity of which could not be foreseen.

Kicki's relationship with her fellow squirrels was always strained. I doubt that even her mate could get more out of her in this respect than a temporary coyness that ended with the consummation of their courtship. Apart from this, whichever one she encountered – the dashing red male or the snub-nosed one, the old female with both ears turned over, or the young sleek one which I suspect was her own daughter – it always upset her no end. Her lower jaw began to waggle as in an excitable old lady, she stamped her hind feet, scolded long and loudly with her snout in the air. If these threats were not enough, she made feigned rushes, accompanied by ferocious gestures. She brooked no opposition. Once she had announced her standpoint, like a pocket-sized lion, she did not hesitate to leap into battle, and she never withdrew until she had made herself thoroughly understood.

This behaviour was obviously a part of the self-preservation pattern established in the red squirrel tribe and was only pronounced at the feeding place, where many squirrels were attracted by ample and accessible food supplies. Through Kicki I found that by studying a red squirrel's reactions and playing up to its natural instincts, its behaviour could be modified and made less offensive. Kicki's capacity for food, she had shown me, was *not* unlimited. But if she were frustrated, either by lack of food, or hindered in reaching it, this touched off the chain reactions in her, which were exasperating to the bird-banding and feeding-station operator. To be a pest was therefore merely an attitude forced upon her by circumstances, an attitude rather commendable than otherwise, in that it showed her invincible spirit. But all trouble was effectually circumvented by the establishment of *several* feeding places for the squirrels at the feeding-station. Very soon the habit-loving little creatures became remarkably faithful to their own feeders and those of the birds were punctiliously left in peace.

So far so good, but in her home territory, Kicki still had a burning question to settle for me. Did the red squirrels rob birds' nests intentionally or accidentally? She gave me her answer at three closely watched nests within her own territory; two of the red-eyed vireo hung in trees and one of the chestnut-sided warbler not a foot-and-a-half from the ground. Both vireo nests delivered all their young safely in due time in spite of the fact that I constantly watched Kicki running around close, but never too close, to these nests. The warbler nest was hung in a raspberry bush in the middle of one of Kicki's main lanes and the day I found it robbed of all its eggs I was in no doubt of the robber's identity. The warblers thereupon moved off 60 feet to the south, well out of Kicki's paths, and there successfully raised three young. Without ill intent apparently, she could not guarantee anything that happened on or in the vicinity of her lanes which, in a light "tracking" snow could be mapped exactly from end to end. After all, who could be blamed for picking a red apple dangled lusciously before the eyes?

As I wrote this, Kicki dropped in through the top of my window looking for peanuts. She found one, gallopped over the keyboard and settled herself comfortably on the carriage to eat it, her tail draped behind her over the typewriter. There she sat, embodying all the truth and falsehoods ever spoken about red squirrels, a rebuke to me and to all mankind for our quickness to persecute animals about whom we have learned only half-truths. She had debunked all my preconceived ideas about her as airily as she swished her tail from one mood to another and had taught me, through the grinding process of association, that all living creatures that co-exist develop adaptations which make it possible for each to fit satisfactorily and profitably into the niches they are meant to occupy in the Great Pattern.

With the arrival at the feeding-station of several litters of young squirrels in late summer, serious problems of over-population often occur. Increased competition always creates intensified nervous tension. The red squirrels are highly strung creatures. Their threshold of tolerance is low.

Relief from stress is contrived by set individual behaviour patterns. One animal takes to chasing the birds from the feeders and unlucky the bird that lets itself be cornered. Another gnaws, tears asunder objects and/or materials in places where food ought to be found. A third one, jealously guarding its favourite feeding spot, with or without provocation turns into a formidable fighter. Its paws held like the hands of a boxer out front, it rises on its hind legs and advances in jerky hops, screaming at the top of its voice. A rush, quick as lightning, ensues and a mêlée, with the antagonists rolling together, somersaulting, tearing at each other's hides. Then, as quickly as the battle began, it dissolves. The trespasser flees and the contender takes a nap. Crowding, over-population, local or general, thus sooner or later initiate conditions and behaviour that force upon the living creatures and their environment the necessary adjustments. And with this comes relief.

The flying squirrel, closely related to the red ones and sharing the same habitat, is entirely different in behaviour and temperament. Nocturnal of habit, the flying squirrel's body is full of folds of skin that extend and support it as it glides spread-eagle from on high. Its fur in shades of grey and white is silky and soft. Its enormous eyes that see in the dark seem to be nothing but bottomless black pupils.

Peace-loving and fun-loving, the flying squirrels are friendly and sociable among themselves. They sleep together on cold nights in the same hole; they happily eat together on the same feeding shelf. They nudge each other, push a bit, chase each other, fall playfully overboard, only to reappear to sit close, close together. Their movements are mercurial, based on instant avoidance and escape, for many dangers threaten them in the dark from owls, foxes, martens, fishers. Not until one day, when I foolishly dabbed a gob of peanut butter on the bare trunk of the great pine, did I realize the risks they run. The night before a great horned owl had been hooting back of the hill. As morning dawned I found five tails – just the flat tails, silky and grey – below the half-eaten peanut butter on the trunk of the pine.

Irrepressible Nuthatch

The amazing thing was not that she came but that she stayed. For, to my knowledge, no other red-breasted nuthatch, except she and her present mate, in those early days, had remained in our study area at Pimisi Bay more than a winter and a spring. After that they usually vanished, and not one of more than 20 banded nuthatches have ever returned. Furthermore, she achieved an unusual performance for one of her kind.

But let me introduce her properly! On December 17, 1952, a day of cloudy skies and frost in the air and six inches of snow on the ground, she arrived unaccompanied by anyone but a flock of black-capped chickadees. I suspect that she met these gay commuters somewhere back in the woods and that she could not resist joining so carefree a company. But when they arrived at the feeding-station at the house, and the chickadees swarmed onto the feeding sticks and hollowed-out coconuts, and began eating of the foods served there – lard pudding, peanut butter, and suet – our nuthatch held back. Never before, I am sure, had she seen such strange contraptions, and if the chickadees had not been pecking at them she would never have recognized their contents as food.

She perched in the white spruce and from this vantage point, her body extended in the longest line from her stubby tail to her up-turned bill, she flickered her wings lightly, gazed down upon the chickadees with keen interest and said, *yep-yep-yep!* But before she could do anything else, the chickadee flock departed upon the next lap of their routine tour – and she with them.

When she appeared upon our scene her plumage was slightly worn. It is true that the females of the species seem to be more subdued in their colouring of blue-grey and rust than the males. But unless the shade of their crowns is seen, shiny black in the males and a soft blue-grey in the females, the sexes cannot be distinguished, especially a few months after the annual moult. Just after the moult, all red-breasted nuthatches look strikingly bright and colourful, but various degrees of wear soon rob them of their good looks. Only the fledgling can be distinguished by its plumage with certainty from its elders. But, in addition to the fluffy and pale feather-dress that adorns it before the change into the first winter plumage, the young bird often wears black spots or small lines on the chin and on the white eyebrow stripe.

It is different with the leg colour of the red-breasted nuthatch. In young birds just out of the nest it is very light greenish-yellow, by comparison distinctly lighter than in the parents. In the old birds I have examined in the hand, it has varied from light olive-green to very dark, almost black. Although the evidence is still far from conclusive, it is possible that leg colour is related to age in this species.

Assuming that this is true, our nuthatch was young, because her legs were light green. In view of her coming at that very time, and alone, this was important. Had she hatched in the summer of that year she might never yet have had a mate. The exciting thing was that three males were already daily visitors at our feeding-station. They had arrived during November, one by one, all without mates. One of them had light green legs, the second, brownish-grey, and the third, almost black legs. I had banded all of them with aluminum bands before the lady appeared; the first one wore a gold and the third a blue band, while the second one was uncoloured. Thus she produced a promising situation for answering my burning questions: Do red-breasted nuthatches, like the white-breasted nuthatches, normally live paired the year around? How do they go about getting paired?

The next day she had successfully overcome all prejudices against food and feeding places that did not look natural to her. Every time she came with her entourage of chickadees she ate voraciously as if in dire need of quick restoration of lost storage fat. Neither this day nor the next were there any signs of an encounter having taken place between her and any one of the three bachelors. All four came and went at staggered periods, each with their separate flock of chickadees.

On the fourth morning it happened. What extraordinary luck that I happened to see her alighting on the wire! She sat, hunched just a little, pointing her bill from side to side and aiming to take off for the nearest suet stick, when *plunk!* Uncoloured Male alighted on the same wire two and a half feet away from her. The jolt startled her. No sooner did she catch sight of the male than she dashed at him, her wings beating the air almost as fast as those of a hummingbird. Obviously, her design was not to fight him, but to sit in the spot where he sat. He flew off, thus reacting to her move as the situation required. Again she flew after him in the same manner, in and out of the thick branches of the white spruce. Twice more she sat herself where he sat, and twice more he gave way to her. As a finale, she perched high above the world on the tip of a branch of the white spruce. There she pointed her bill rhythmically from side to side and lifted her wings high vertically above her back, flapping them up and down in time with the movements of her bill. If she said anything during this demonstration I was too far away to hear it.

I did not see any more displays until shortly afterward, when she and Uncoloured Male came to the feeding-station together. He alighted on the suet stick first, upside down, fed, then bent his head far back and gazed in the direction where she was, uttering soft notes, *tetetete*. I looked at her and there she was, pivoting slowly from side to side like an electric fan in action, while she pointed her bill toward him and shivered her wings as she answered him with the same soft notes, *tetetete*. Thus she dispelled all my doubts of their happy union.

For several reasons her behaviour was interesting. First, because she, not the male, took the initiative, although it is known that in some species the females may undertake the first pairing gestures very early or just before the nesting season actually starts. Second, if, as it appeared to be, this was her first meeting with one of the bachelors, she did no choosing but opened procedures with the first and the best that might become her mate. How she recognized him as a male is a third question. Did she, as we do, know his black crown as his badge of masculinity? Perhaps, knowing him only for a nuthatch, she simply flew at him to see what he would do. Very often, during the off-season, the males are inclined to evade the females; but a female might have stood up to her. After her initial move, she confirmed the male's attitude by two more "attacks" and, finally, she performed a "victory" ritual on the branch of the white spruce.

Once paired, the couple became a close unit. I agree fully with Viscount Grey of Fallodon, who wrote: "The birds that mate for life and remain together throughout the year evidently get a high degree of satisfaction from each other's company...."

Undoubtedly this was true about my pair. It was constantly demonstrated by their mutual concern for each other and close attendance upon each other; by the female's pretty attitudes before her mate, with wings ashivering as a prelude to coming courtship feeding; and by their unceasing conversation amongst themselves – *tetetete*.

One day when the pair was feeding at a stick, a chickadee tried to dislodge them. Uncoloured Male ominously raised himself to his full height on stretched legs, clinging precariously to the stick with the tips of his claws. High above his back he lifted his fully opened wings and in this pose he pivoted in a half-circle back and forth, like a ballerina on tiptoe. The striking display he thus attained of feathers and colour patterns and the amazing enlargement of the midget nuthatch soon robbed the chickadee of all desire to interfere.

On January 5, 1953, the little female went into one of my bird-banding traps. I put an aluminum band on her left leg, and a green band on her right one. Thus she acquired a name – A for aluminum, G for green – Aggie.

Early in March, Uncoloured Male began to sing. The song of the red-breasted nuthatch is far from impressive, musically. It is a continuous, weak-sounding, one-note *we-we-we-we-we*, that can hardly be heard more than 50 feet away. But there is a quality in this tonal effort and the manner in which it is given that makes it remarkable. There he sat, Aggie's mate, atop the tall white spruce. He held his body in a straight horizontal line and grasped his perch with legs well apart while he swayed rhythmically from side to side, the notes pouring freely from his slender wide-opened bill in all directions.

It was not a territorial song he gave, in the sense that other birds advertise their territories, for he was far from the spot which, I later found, the pair had selected for their nesting. But apart from the nest area, the nuthatch also establishes a secondary territory which he guards and defends with utmost vigilance. This is an irregularly circular space in the midst of which his mate has her being, and which, therefore, moves along with the birds. Nor does he, like many other birds, need to make himself conspicuous in order to attract the opposite sex, since long ago he acquired his mate. For that very brief period in the spring during which the nuthatch sings, I think that he performs mostly from pure enjoyment, even though other elements, like appeal to his mate or the edification of other nuthatch males, may play a role.

A few days later, Uncoloured Male fed his mate before me. Aggie was half-crouched on the wire, with her neck stretched forward and her bill pointing slowly from side to side. With very small movements she shivered her wings rapidly. The male at a feeding stick grasped a morsel in his bill, flew to the wire, hopped toward her in a businesslike manner, and popped it into her bill. At that moment he acquired a new name – Hop-hop-hop. She, having swallowed his spousal offering, flew to the stick and began gorging herself on lard pudding. Sometimes courtship feeding is not a need but a ritual.

A week later Hop-hop-hop sat on the very tip of the dead white birch. It was an overcast morning in the middle of March, with a chill wind blowing from the east and 11 inches of snow still on the ground. But there he was, obviously in a state of ecstasy, pivoting back and forth, lightly flicking his wings, and singing at the top of his small voice. Then I discovered the hole above which he serenaded. Six inches below him, only just started, it was nothing but a mere indication of beginning hole-boring marked on the white bark. The next instant Aggie clung to the spot and began working diligently.

In cavity-nesting species, the hole-boring period is usually an arduous time filled with work and little play, and only toward the end of it love-making comes to the fore. Only on that account can I explain Aggie's reserve when, a few days later, I met the pair mid-way between the feeding-station and the nesting place. As Hop-hop-hop tried to advance toward her, all his body elongated, pointed and extended forward, she turned away and would not suffer him to approach. His amorous attempt thwarted, he retired to a nearby tree and here, his head stretched toward her and his whole body swaying violently from side to side with wings vibrating rapidly at his sides, he suddenly passed over from his continuous *tetetetete* into a high-pitched, meaningful, trilled note and held it for a long second. The next instant both birds were gone in the direction of the nest. How beautifully and smoothly nature can relieve and divert the high tension of an unfulfilled desire!

Until the end of April I had too few moments to watch the pair and I saw little of them. Once, finding no pitch smeared around the hole I felt sure that the nest was abandoned. Then one day I found the pair in their favourite feeding place not far from the nest tree. Obviously, it was a recess during incubation and Aggie was travelling about from tree to tree. She picked little food by herself, as her mate kept feeding her with inexhaustible solicitude. From time to time he interrupted his services and mounted the nearest tree-top whence, assuming his customary pose of musical abandon, he sang to her his sweetest songs, *we-we-we-we-we*.

I followed them to the nest and was surprised to find that, with eggs evidently being incubated, no pitch had yet been applied around the doorway. Hitherto, eggs in the nest and pitch around the doorway had been almost simultaneous phenomena in all the cases I had watched. In fact, I had become accustomed to regard pitch as the only sure sign of occupancy in the early stages of a nesting.

But a week later, when every sign and calculation indicated that the chamber within was full of newly hatched babies, gumdrops glistened around the nest opening for the first time. Hop-hop-hop came with food and with a graceful flourish disappeared directly into the small aperture. An instant later he flitted out; in his bill he carried a tiny white fecal sac, which he carefully put away on a twig. Aggie followed him closely. As she flew after him low over my head, she gave a song composed of a string of soft, clear, utterly musical notes, an astonishing and never-before-heard performance by a red-breasted nuthatch female.

While they were gone, the gum around the entrance to their nest gleamed and sparkled in the sun, like eyes can sparkle in the refraction of light. For eyes in nature, whether live or imagined, as they may appear in a pattern or as light strikes an object or a substance, seem to have a discouraging effect upon would-be trouble-makers.

On June 5, Aggie and her mate conducted their brood of fluffy children to the feeding-station for the first time. The youngsters were fast adapting themselves to conditions outside their secluded hole nest. By trial and error they were learning to recognize food, pecking at stuff like their parents did and every so often getting a good piece of "meat" quite on their own. A few days later, father brought four of them to the bird-bath. It was a hot day. He followed his habit – hop-hop-plop – and then abandoned himself to a series of vigorous splashes and duckings, the spray flying. The young ones sat in a row on the edge of the bath. They put their bills into the water and with great energy and aptitude went through the movement of ducking and wing-shivering without getting a single drop of water sparkling over their plumages. Only after a good deal of "air-bathing" did the full ritual gradually dawn upon them. Before they were little more than two weeks out of the nest, all were independent of their parents. Anyway, Aggie had long since ceased bothering about them, but the significance of this remained to be discovered.

The time passed and the pair was still around, rugged-looking and worn, but curiously without signs of getting into heavy moult. One day early in July, to my surprise I perceived Hop-hop-hop atop his dead birch above the old nest-hole, going through his usual ritual of wing-flicking and bill-pointing as when he was at the height of nesting. Then he flew in and out of the nest – and I thought he did that just from old habit. But, no, a few days later the signs became too obvious to doubt the true state of affairs. *Aggie and her mate were raising a second brood in the same nest in the same season.* There seems to be no other record of a red-breasted nuthatch having raised a second brood in the same season, although, obviously, it can and must have happened before. Its European counterpart, *Sitta europaea affinis*, is said to have "one brood usually, but exceptionally two."

On July 22, exactly four months and seven days after the nuthatches had delivered their first excavating peck on the entrance into their nest-to-be, I watched their last son launch himself upon his first flight. He was sitting in the opening, calling with his scrapy little note, *yan-yan-yan*, to his brothers and sisters already hidden in the tall trees 100 feet away. He pushed himself far out. Of a sudden he was airborne, successfully bucking a 15 m.p.h. side wind. He landed safely in the crown of a birch 80 feet from the nest. And the repeated calling from juvenile throats told the parents and me the precise location of four young birds that had just left the nest-hole.

There is not much more to tell about Aggie, except that she kept on feeding this last brood long past the customary two weeks. Naturally, the youngsters, now a lot fatter and heavier than she, continued to pursue her as long as she serviced them until, finally, the moult wrung from her all her available energies.

Hop-hop-hop disappeared at this time, and I am certain that nothing but death could have forced this separation from his mate. The former bachelor with a blue band on one of his black legs, having lost his partner a few weeks earlier, still came to the feeding-station. I missed that meeting between him and Aggie, when their courtship must have begun. But the moment I heard again the pretty mutual note, *tetetetete*, I knew that nature, once more, had appropriately adjusted two nuthatch lives.

Part Six

Bird Migration –
Still an Enigma

Many are the theories, manifold the methods of research that have been and still are employed to penetrate into the riddles of bird migration. Much has been learned. The birds' extraordinary sense of orientation, of finding their way across continents, so many of them returning precisely to the place where they came from, the inexperienced young bird travelling alone for the first time but finding the way traditional for its species, the birds' sensitivity for temperature and the weather, are known facts. But the origin of bird migration, how it started, and the workings of each bird's inner drive and the exact guide directing its travel, are questions still largely unanswered.

On this 46th parallel most of the woodland song-birds are migrants. Consider the time out of each year in the lives of these birds taken up by their migrations alone from north to south and back! Although banding and technology have succeeded in monitoring some fast passages of single birds – hundreds of miles in one single night – the average time involved, with stops for feeding and resting, must be quite considerable.

What we see of true bird migration in this region may extend practically from February into December. Birds from the far north, such as the snowy, boreal and hawk owls, the northern shrikes, the redpolls and the snow buntings, here reach the northernmost part of their wintering grounds. Migrations of birds occur also in the depth of winter, but these movements are mostly local or regional and concern habitual winter residents moving from one place to another in search of fresh food supplies among the thinly distributed resources.

When the effect of the sun's travel northwards becomes noticeable, the wintering redpolls and snow buntings, and with them the owls and the shrikes, begin to show restlessness. In large flocks the small birds move about, often escorted by a predator owl or shrike. We note marked influxes of these birds in step-ladder fashion, here one, two, three days, perhaps longer, then gone, whirling out over the lake northwards. At this early date a flow of milder air may even tempt a crow to cover a section of the northward route later to be retraced should the weather turn cold again.

Then comes March, with its spring-winter storms alternating with thaws and warmer winds. Strong and very bright sunshine falls on the piles of snow, warming the earth underneath them. Sparkling rivulets trickle down the slopes, seemingly gentle but later with a compulsory eroding force that is apt to carry away everything before them. The northern birds now all gone, the early migrants from the south appear. These are the sturdy and tough birds sufficiently omnivorous to tolerate the vicissitudes of the fickle March and early April weather. Once the stream of northbound migrants has been fully turned on, it goes on spasmodically according to the wandering weather fronts, to reach its peak volume in late May, while the latest of the migrants continue to arrive well into the first week of June.

If, during the frantically busy breeding season, there is a respite when all migratory movement ceases, it is exceedingly short. By the end of June or early July some of the shore birds breeding in the far north begin to move southward. Gradually the returning flocks of birds increase in volume to flow southward until, by December when the lakes are dead and the first snow is already on the ground, the last straggler has come and gone.

Flight South

August 24, 1948, was a rainy morning. A warm front was passing across the land bringing cloud, rain and thunder-storms. After the front has passed, in the natural schedule of weather changes a cold front is due with the wind blowing from the north or north-west. Today the tree swallows are moving and, standing by an open lake, I watch them passing in review. They are flying in an unbroken stream, many hundreds, perhaps thousands if all of them could be seen and counted, the whole mass of them gliding slowly due south. They fly leisurely, whirling and twisting in their course, feeding as they go. Some of them are flying so high among the clouds that they appear as mere specks, others are skimming low across the water of the lake. Their flight is an alternating series of rapid wing-beats and short sailing intervals on stiff wings. Every so often some of them double back to join dense gatherings of swallows foraging in pockets of cloud, where, presumably, swarms of insects attract them. Swallow notes come to me from on high, weakly but unceasingly, *tritt-tritt-tritt*.

Forty minutes have elapsed and the swallows are still coming out of the north, passing, whirling, and disappearing. The thunderclouds gather and thicken, and still the swallows are coming. But now the streams are beginning to thin, until in the end only stragglers flying fast to catch up come by in pouring rain. Low, but with the same elegance and speed as the first ones flew more than an hour ago, the late ones whirl and circle with their broad mouths wide open to catch the flying mites under the darkening clouds. Then, suddenly, it was all over, the sky empty.

A few days later in the late afternoon another great migrating flock of barn swallows and tree swallows sat resting on the telephone wires along the road. There were hundreds of them and the wires sagged under their combined weight. To the accompaniment of twittering music, the swallows moved, pushed lightly, flew off, and returned, to meet musical protests and a bit of pushing and adjusting to make room for all. New flocks arrive and join the others. For nearly a mile the swallows spread out along the wires, a free, open, beautifully accessible perching place accommodating so many, and with room for still more of them, as they assemble where at first only a few found the convenient anchorage.

Three years later. I got up and went out early. It was dark, no moon, not even the faintest line of light at the horizon. Only a few stars shimmered through wisps of mist, paling, announcing the break of dawn.

All was still. The pines stood tall and silent around me, magnificently outlined against the sky, like dark, benevolent sentinels on guard over my small house. I heard the muffled beats of my own heart. In the intense stillness I felt the pulse of that which is immortal.

Then came the sound. With my face turned skyward I stood waiting. I heard it again. It was the faint call of a bird overhead in the dark, flying south. Again and again it came, from near, from afar, moving from distance to distance up there in the unseen – bird calling to bird.

I tried to recognize the calls. But the voices of migrating birds in the air sound strangely unfamiliar. Perhaps the distance and the night distort them, or perhaps the birds' migratory calls are special and different. The whistle of a thrush came to me, shorter, softer, it seemed, than its notes on the ground, and poised, as if expecting an answer that soon came from another and yet another thrush. Then a brief utterance with a nasal twang interrupted the thrushes' conversations; it could scarcely have come from any other than a tiny short-tailed red-breasted nuthatch. Then, unmistakably, a white-throated sparrow sought an answer to its long-drawn, sibilant *tseet*.

Light began to show at the horizon and seeped in among the trees as the sea creeps in among the dunes at flood-tide. This was the signal for the birds to come down. They circled, searched for safe landfalls somewhere in the tapering silhouettes of the tree-tops. Seconds later I knew they had made it and that they now sat in safety with their feet curled tight around a twig. I knew because their calls no longer moved from place to place but became stationary and louder.

Though I could not see them yet, I fancied that the birds were preening themselves during their short rest before the light became strong enough for them to begin feeding. What more natural act for a bird just alighting from a night-long flight! How comforting to ruffle the plumage with a vigorous shrug and then to smooth each feather back into place! From their dawn perches, the birds called and called across the twilight woods.

As I stood listening to them, of a sudden the meaning and importance of the voice to the migrating bird struck me as never before.

Whatever may be the mainspring that starts and maintains the impulsion of avian migration, once on the wing there can be little doubt but that the bird possesses in its voice a pilot for itself and its fellows as accurate and reliable as a radio beam. On their nocturnal flights, small woodland birds seldom, if ever, fly in tight flocks or formations and they have no slip-stream from the bird next ahead to follow. Nor is sight one of their chief guides in the dark. Instead, flying in loose gatherings, one by one, tiny specks between earth and cloud, these birds seek contact with each other, feel for guidance from their lone and lofty positions, with their faint but penetrating voices. It may be supposed that the bird whirled off the beaten track, inland or out to sea, is lost chiefly because it has lost earshot contact with its fellows. Aimlessly it flies off the beam, until once more it hears the voices of other birds and joins them to save its life. Or else, in the end, it drops earthwards, exhausted, in utter loneliness.

The sun arose upon a forest flecked with gold. The leaves were turning and their brilliant colours brightened the spaces between the evergreens with an unbelievably lucent effect. A puff of the morning breeze dropped showers of dead needles from the branches of the pines and they accumulated on the ground into a springy light-brown carpet.

The birds that came down at dawn moved on. Soon they were followed by wave after wave of migrating warblers and other woodland species, which for brief moments took possession of a piece of the forest. On northern and north-western slopes they usually came to earth and then flew on over the land, from bush to bush and from tree to tree, along preferred topographical landmarks, streams, lake shores, ridges or valleys. Unimportant corners of some roadside or forest edge would suddenly seethe with birds, as a larger concentration of them spilled over the margins of habitual trails and spread out in search of food.

Some days when the birds sensed the coming of a cold air mass, they lingered and fed assiduously, needing, above all, to maintain their resistance and strength against whatever hardships might be in store for them. Generally each species kept to the levels at which they were accustomed to forage. Nevertheless, there were endless rivalries over space. In swift zigzag chases or by aerial dueling that took the combatants aloft, bill to bill, and then dropped them apart like two falling leaves, the invisible limits of the feeding areas that surrounded each bird and to which, by natural law, no other was entitled, were often vigorously contested.

At favourable moments in sheltered places and in sunshine,

birds sang. Often their songs were off-key, raspy and fragmentary, as if their voices, unused during the post-nuptial moult, needed a great deal of practise in order to regain their tone at the revival of song in autumn. Sometimes a thrush, a wren, or a warbler, having once more achieved its full vocal powers, gave a song that seemed sweeter to me than any sung in the spring, because it was not expected, or because, perhaps, the bird was expressing its sheer joy in being alive.

At other times, especially during warm days that might precede the onset of a cold spell, the migrant birds often streamed through the woods, like shooting stars streaking through the skies of an August night. To cover ground seemed to be their main concern. On and on at all costs, no time to stop and feed, no time to linger and play, time only to move, to hasten southwards mile after mile, over roads, along rivers, valleys and ridges.

As I stood watching them in these breathless moments, almost unable to move from the fascination of the ceaseless movement around me, I often wondered how these small woodland birds could stand the pace set by their own relentless impulse to go south. The next instant, my eyes fastened upon a twig in a sheltered corner. There a lone yellow-throat perched between two leaves which, exactly like the plumage of the bird itself, shifted from green to a golden bright yellow. The bird was fast asleep, blissfully oblivious of speed, food and nightly travels.

On a mission in which weather, speed and food were the vital factors, sleep was, perhaps, only a secondary matter. A little nap aside that took the bird out of the moving flock for 10 or 15 minutes seemed quite adequate. I watched the yellow-throat stir, awaken wide-eyed, and with a little shrug, move on in the wake of the last straggler of its flock.

The blue jays and the woodpeckers took scant notice of the passing migrants, perhaps because they themselves were in a nomadic mood. The chickadees behaved differently. Scarcely a flock of migrating birds moved through the woods without their escort of chickadees which with chatter and song left no one in doubt of their existence.

It was difficult to decide whether the effusive chickadees

attracted the migrants, or whether the passing strangers aroused some latent urges in the chickadee heart that lured the two parties together. Either might be true. Perhaps it was an alternating affair, governed by circumstances. At any rate, both groups continually announced their conviviality by actions and voice and this penchant for fraternization was indeed a part of each individual's prerequisite for survival. What eventually caused them to part company remained a mystery, and where it happened, a flexible point; but my bird bands on the legs of the chickadees proved that they stayed within a certain territory while the migrating birds moved onwards.

The movement of the migrants decreased with the coming of noon and usually became mere trickles, or ceased altogether during the afternoon and early evening. This traceless disappearance of large numbers of birds after midday gave me cause for endless speculation. Going out of my territory they must enter another region, just as when leaving a neighbouring territory they must come into my region if it were in their path. But the birds disappeared from everywhere. Where did they go? Where did they hide? Even at the end of the day, when they vanished into thin air, it was certainly never from any point where I might be afforded the thrill of seeing the nightly take-off of a single bird.

Presently, as the rotund face of a harvest or hunter's moon rose from behind the hills and mirrored itself in the surface of the lake, I trained my glasses upon that golden disc to see what was going on within its path of illumination. Now and again a bird flitted across my field of vision. In half an hour I counted 26 birds which passed ghost-like across the face of the moon on wings of silver, only a fraction of the numbers in the air that night.

What matchless courage these winged creatures possess, what firm reliance upon the equity of the Law! For them there is no going back, no hesitation, but up, out, and away.

Leaning against the bulwark of my house, I stood there earthbound with my feet fast to the rock, envying the wild bird its fantastic flight in the night, and above all the integrity of its impulse.

And there were others too. Those early days provided

spectacles of many migrations, all different and strikingly sensational. Often in the spring the warbler migrations brought veritable inundations of these brightly coloured masterpieces of nature's creation. They filled every greening tree all of a sudden, poured in over the land with twitter and song, unceasing movement, uncountable in their great numbers, driven by their relentless urge to reach the hallowed spot, the set end of their flight somewhere within each species' traditional breeding range.

The spring migrations are the most dangerous. The fickle weather of spring poses problems. Too strong and persistent flows of warm air lure many migrants too far north, there to be hit by the following cold front. Many die from hunger and exposure. Many more survive – the strong, the powerful, the food-finders and the adaptable – to carry out the task of propagation quickly, excitedly, successfully, during the next three short months.

Then on the move again, back southwards, most of the adult warblers and some of the others, the red tanager males among them, in changed plumages of less flamboyant design, similar to the dress of the new generation, of the immatures, in discreetly subdued colours of greenish greys and browns to better match the autumnal background. Travel is easier in the fall. Now no longer does the weather create harsh obstacles to be met head on. Instead north-to-south tail winds are apt to push migrants on into the warmer zones for the winter, leaving our forest empty.

On a late September day, the glories of the autumn colours are already about to fade, and the grey clouds during and after a cold front scud across the sky on a north wind! Then the first flight of snowy and Canada geese are to be seen on their way south. Soon my binoculars discern one V or line formation after the other, crossing the sky, flock upon flock flying just under the clouds. The air fills with loud honking in their respective jargons. After such a day, to see a flock of geese, illuminated by the slanting orange rays of the setting sun shining through a slit in the near overcast, coming down on a lonely lake with wings flapping, legs down, amid a chorus of excited voices shredding the silence, this is a sight and a sound never to be forgotten.

Looking back over the records, I now realize that the early 1950s saw the initial changes that eventually were to herald the decline in numbers of certain species of birds. Unnoticed at first, the decline became discernible gradually with some assurance.

Never have swallows been seen in such numbers as in those early years. Only comparatively minor flights may on occasion be spotted by an observer lucky enough to find himself in the right place at the right time. A decade hence, will even these have vanished to leave the air undisturbed, full of insects and pollution?

And the large warbler migrations that used to fill the last weeks of May with such colour and movement and thrills in our endeavours to follow them – to see and to hear them sing and to find them spread out along our forest edges and into our forest, nesting – where have they gone? Why have these streams of birds become so thin? Oh, they are still there! There are still flights to be seen when suddenly the branches of the trees begin to move with birds alighting and taking off, going northwards, but not by far with the same frequency, nor with as large gatherings as were to be seen 30 years ago. For the changes caused by the constantly shrinking natural habitats, not only on land but also in the air, with the widespread increase of high towers built, and aerials of all kinds and heights, are destructive to these migrating birds. So here, too, the question arises: For how long will our northern forests harbour this diminishing brilliantly coloured throng of insectivorous birds that return in the spring in numbers sufficient not only to contribute to the maintenance of the natural balances between insects and plants, but also to survive and to reproduce?

Consider only the one single fact that during a recent fall migration at one lone lighthouse on an island in the Georgian Bay, a keen observer, who spent a week there to study migration, found a total of 3,150 birds of 49 species killed at night during that week. Of these, 1,083 were Swainson's thrushes and 498 ovenbirds. On the nights of the highest kills the sound of the birds hitting the lighthouse and the guy wires was at times like heavy rain.

Then multiply this with the number of birds similarly destroyed against comparable obstacles, accounts of which are frequent in the literature across the North American continent throughout the recent decade! True, the replacement capacity of nature is enormous. But the conclusion that the effect is negligible, that these vulnerable birds will stage a come-back without any change in the trends of causative circumstances needs no computer to reject.

So what is there left? There are always compensations. Among mine are the ruby-throated hummingbirds, these tiny birds with their miniature feathers, their curved bills of finest dimensions, the iridescence of the contrasting colours of ruby, black, white and green, one of nature's most exquisite creations. It seems almost an incongruous anomaly that so delicate a bird, originating in the tropics and living on nectar sucked from flowers, should belong to and thrive in so harsh and rough a haunt as this cool beautiful land. But from May into September here they are at home. Even before the flowers are in bloom they arrive on humming wing-beats, hovering at the window, hovering around the aspen catkins, only to buzz off, whence – farther north . . . amazing dash, fantastic élan!

Our sugar-water fountains are out, and it is impossible to deny the identity of the returned bird. There he is, the male with his gorgeous ruby gorget shifting to night-black as the light falls, flying directly to the place where the sugar-water was to be found last year. A few days later the female arrives in gleaming green plumage all over her head and back, to her white-spotted, as if pearl-edged, tail.

Elfin confrontations and lightning pursuits ensue, while the weight loss from their long journey from the Central Americas is being eagerly recovered at the opening blossoms and the sweet liquid containers. The pair are soon engaged in courtship, the male wooing the female in a swinging rhythmic performance that carries him high up in the air and deep down, possessively aggressive, while she remains elusive.

In the impetuosity of his display he flies against the

window, a glancing blow, and falls stunned. I pick him up – he revives and grasps my finger tight. Then just sits for well over an hour. I take him to the sugar-water container. He finds the tiny hole at once, inserts his bill and with his long serpentine tongue laps up long draughts of the sweet liquid. I expect him to leave, but for 10 minutes more his tight grip is still on my finger. Then the tiny bird lifts, for a second hovers, confronting me – and is off.

In late July the young are out. There follows a period of a great amount of dashing around among the three, two young and the mother, accompanied by excited stridulous notes. The female brings honeyed feedings to the young on the wires, beautifully performed on the wing. The male, having done nothing all summer but buzzing and feeding after fulfilling his part of the partnership, now hovers frequently at the sweet drink fountain at the window. He is still there drinking on August 25, in the morning. Then, suddenly, I see him go, he and another, through the opening in the trees in a bee-line due south across the lake . . .

For another week the female lingers, she and one of the young ones. They spend the morning drinking frequently. This presages nothing as they have done that every morning of late.

I didn't see them go – but suddenly there is emptiness.

Cold Spring

The winter at Pimisi Bay in 1976 had not been too severe. When January came the snow was only a foot and a half deep. The taller weeds, even the evening primroses, were sticking their heads above the snow with their pods full of seeds – reason enough for the redpolls to stay over and spend a few days clinging to the bountiful food resource.

The deer too had benefitted. With the snow not so deep, more browse was available. A late January thaw with freezing rain put a crust on top of the snow, hard enough in open places to support the deer and make their movements easier. A pair of them, a buck and a doe, judging by their tracks, elected to spend the rest of the winter within our premises. Some previous memory, no doubt, prompted the doe one night to come right up to the house to feast on two small cedars which we had nursed with great care into rich voluminous shapes. To do this had taken us years, for the white cedar, the *arbor vitae* of the north, is a slow-growing tree.

More snow came in February. But the crust left from the January thaw prevented the new accumulation from becoming a significant impediment to movement. The additional snow suited the ruffed grouse fine, for it likes to burrow down into the soft insulating stuff to sleep during cold winter nights. But the refuges of nature's creatures are seldom foolproof. Occasionally a roving predator, a red fox or a short-tailed weasel with an empty stomach to drive it sniffs its way to the grouse's hiding place. And the bird's sudden explosion, literally into the face of danger, may not be of sufficient force to divert the famished animal from its purpose. To one hapless grouse this was what happened, and only the hollow in the snow with a few grouse droppings and a heap of soft feathers beside it were left to tell the tale. It is true, of course, that the fox and the weasel must also eat, and the balance of chance favouring predator or prey is extremely finely adjusted.

During the first week of February a lone redpoll strayed into our territory. No doubt the presence of this bird later led a roaming band of other redpolls – birds usually of the more open spaces – to the feeding-station tucked under the trees in the tall forest. They found sunflower seeds and cracked corn to be a highly palatable diet. One day a trespassing ruffed grouse, a female in the rare red-phase plumage, happened to sample the corn strewn out for the redpolls. After that she made it a habit to come every day, snow or shine. She had wide experience in how to find buried treasures; she ploughed her way through the snow, scratching and picking the corn pellets where no one else could find them. She liked to be alone when engaged in this business, and she was well schooled in the tough game of self-protection. Her feathers raised in display to impress the would-be attacker with her voluminous size effectively kept the red squirrel at bay. The irascible animal could assert itself in her presence only when it happened to take her by surprise.

A prolonged unseasonable thaw with several frost-free nights ushered in March. Spring, the blissful, so long awaited season, seemed to be just around the corner. And, sure enough, the brief warm spell lured the first crow and starling to earlier-than-usual arrivals. The flocks of redpolls began moving northward, back to their subarctic and arctic breeding grounds. They invaded the forest feeding place in great numbers. Tiny dark spots on the white snow, they picked the corn for dear life and other items torn from the trees by the winter winds and now re-emerged in the thaw. Entrancing volatile sprites they were in their striped attire and red caps, and the males more or less daubed with red all down their breasts. Another kind of redpoll would sometimes accompany these flocks, the hoary redpoll, with a pure white rump and what appeared to be "frosted" edges on the feathers. All of them were constantly on the *qui vive*. Now here, assiduously picking the corn; the next instant, on the least or no provocation at all, the whole flock would in one concerted move dash for cover, only a minute later to come dribbling back, one by one, eager to resume the interrupted meal at the same place.

These birds needed to be on the alert. A northern shrike with a sharp eye and hooked beak was also travelling northwards. What was more natural than that it should follow the delectable redpolls! The shrike also needed sustenance to survive. But a pursuer, however adept, could not so easily come by its dinner from these mercurial flocks of flighty redpolls incessantly dashing into thick cover.

After the first indulgence in thaws and showers, stormy weather returned to shroud the infant month of March in deep drifts. The wintry conditions obliterated every early sign of spring and the forest stood white with heavily drooping branches. This is what it looked like. But, deep down, inconvertible stirrings were at work.

On March 17, a heavy snowfall entirely blanched the sun's latest attempts at honeycombing the exposed drifts. A black bear chose that day to emerge from its winter cave, leaving its flat-footed tracks all down our path. Obviously famished, the animal now and again veered off the trail to paw under the low branches of several young balsam firs, lest a morsel of food was to be gleaned from the nearly bare earth underneath the trees.

The first days of April once again turned tantalizingly springlike, and joyous expectations repossessed our hearts.

Killdeer, red-winged blackbirds, brown-headed cowbirds proved welcome harbingers of the blessed season. A few dark-eyed juncos and tree sparrows made hurried empty-bellied appearances ahead of a new fierce cold front descending from the north-west. Again winter gripped the land with frosty nights and snow. The ice on the lake showed no sign of breaking up. Starved blackbirds darkened the feeding-station, taking up most of the room and gulping down the seeds and the corn, leaving the redpolls to find whatever they could in a hurry by dashing in and out among the dark masses.

About the middle of April the weather warmed up slightly to bring an eastern phoebe and a tree swallow earlier than scheduled. But, again, a fierce cold front followed and, watching them, we wondered anxiously whether they would find enough insectivorous fare. Could they sustain life in the spots where the warmth lingered near the ground, or along the shores and over the ice? After them, suddenly released by the balmier winds, a northbound flight of tree sparrows appeared overnight. Though their migration schedules coincide, this dainty sparrow with its rufous cap and dark spot in the centre of the breast, whose summer home is at the far northern tree limits, was never a numerous companion of the forest-dwelling junco. But on this occasion the tree sparrows appeared in numbers never before recorded. They overran the feeding place, fighting their private intraspecific battles, and letting their clear sweet warbles grace the chilly and often gloomy environment.

The third week in April at last saw narrow rifts of black water opening down the middle of the lake. A week later, the melting snow pouring down the slopes provided a springtime high-water crest that wrenched the solid mass of ice free from the grip of the shores. Once uprooted, the ice turned grey-green and quickly began to break up into big floating flakes. A few common mergansers, the drakes resplendent in black and white with sparkling red bills and feet, and a pair of dainty buffleheads, she with a white spot on the cheek, he adorned with a puffy white pom-pom on top of the head, quickly zeroed in onto the open pools between the floes. Flocks of tree swallows, just arrived, coursed across ice and water with open mouths, their reflections racing them with intermittent precision, bellysides up.

The last days of April still did not bring warm weather in spite of a thunderstorm and a shower. But on April 28 the female phoebe, having joined the male the day before, carried the first mud pellet to her old nest on the shelf between our windows.

Frost and snowflurries introduced the gladsome month of May. Six days later an unseasonable storm dumped almost 10 inches of snow upon the land. The forest stood white once again and the mid-winter aspect lasted, unmelting, for three whole days. Hunger struck the birds. Flocks of earlier arrivals and already dispersed residents returned to the feeding-station, and the travelling migrants came down from the skies. The place turned into a tumultuous foregathering area for all the blackbirds of the neighbourhood. A flock of 30 evening grosbeaks reappeared from nowhere and, crowding on a single table, were now too busy cracking sunflower seeds with their stout apple-green bills to swish their tails in courtship. Among them were two purple finch cocks in full breeding regalia, shining amid their yellow companions in the reflected lights of the snow, jewels of burnished copper and magenta. A second unusually belated influx of juncos filled forest and roadsides by the hundreds, together with other sparrows – including a red fox sparrow, snow and debris flying under its vehemently scratching feet. In select places burred-up robins and hermit thrushes added their numbers to this extraordinary invasion of birds. Chilled to the bone, they hopped dismally around, looking for a bare spot where a leaf turned up might yield an iced snail or a leech. At the water's edge, clinging to straws, a few brightly coloured fluffed balls of yellow-rumped warblers tenaciously clung to life, picking gnats and flies that in the relative tepidity of the shore environment revealed their presence.

How the phoebe pair, insect-eaters as they were, survived this prolonged period of snow and gelidity is a mystery. But when, on the fourth day, the clouds broke and the sun briefly peeped forth, the female appeared and busily tucked a bit of lining into the refurbished nest.

Cold and cloudy weather, often with white night frosts, persisted well into the middle of May. The buds on the trees remained stubbornly closed. Meanwhile, the first stragglers of the later migrants, thinly scattered, descended upon the unwelcoming land, all late except a bright male ruby-throated hummingbird. The tiny bird arrived five days after the storm, nine days ahead of its normal vernal appearance, most likely enticed to make the risky advance by the flocks of other migrants streaming across the land. Finding no nectar-filled blossoms, it clung to the furry staminate catkins of the aspens feeding on the pollen, then irrepressibly buzzed off on its precarious journey northwards.

Six days later, after an inordinately prolonged nest-building and honeymoon period spanning a 20- instead of a normal 10-day period, the phoebe laid her first egg in the refitted nest. At the same time, two weeks late, the first dandelion and sweet white violet came into bloom, and the leaf buds of the aspens began at last to break open, spreading a fine veiling of tender green over the forest groves.

Then the miracle happened. Like a dammed river suddenly bursting through the restraining barrier, the mainstream of the late migrants, flycatchers, thrushes, vireos, warblers and rose-breasted grosbeaks poured across the land, staging an invasion such as we had not seen for many, many years. Through the tree-tops along the river, a flight of least flycatchers marked their path by ejaculated passwords – *chebec, chebec*. A pewee's soft notes, all but forgotten, sounded from a bare twig above. Kingbirds, great crested and olive-sided flycatchers suddenly were where they had not been before, adding their characteristic vocalizations to the rising concert of the forest. Ovenbirds, punctuating their passage with song, threaded their way unseen through the undergrowth and from every spot where there was water the water thrushes gave their emphatic rippling melodies. Suddenly the naked trees were alive with brightly adorned warblers, feeding, singing, flitting northward without return. And the sight and the movement recalled into vivid actuality the scenes of the years antedating the poison sprays, when the air was undisturbed by any sounds other than nature's own modulated and syncopated orchestrations; when the now silent spring peepers, toads and leopard frogs mingled their bell-like notes, groans and liquid trills with the inimitable music of the birds.

The amazing streams of migrating birds continued through May 21, 22 and 23. Then it was all over. And the residue of these migrants settled, as sparingly dispersed as they had been found upon their traditional territories in recent years. Left to us was nothing but a memory, an experience recaptured ever so briefly, with the unforgettable songs and sights I knew so well momentarily reclaimed.